A STRING of PEARLS

Wisdom for Productive People

JOHN W. STANKO

A String of Pearls
by John W. Stanko
Copyright © 2014 John W. Stanko

All rights reserved. This book is protected under the copyright laws of the United States of America. This book may not be copied or reprinted for commercial gain or profit. Unless otherwise identified, Scripture quotations are taken from *THE HOLY BIBLE: New International Version* ©**1978 by the New York International Bible Society, used by permission of Zondervan Bible Publishers. All rights reserved.**

Note: all bold text in Bible quotations are author's emphasis.

ISBN 978-1-63360-000-3
For Worldwide Distribution
Printed in the U.S.A.

PurposeQuest Ink
P.O. Box 8881 · Pittsburgh, PA 15221-0881
412.646.2780

INTRODUCTION

If you haven't noticed, I am a devotional junkie - not to reading them, but to writing them! It all started in 1996 when I wrote what came to be known as *A Daily Dose of Proverbs*. Then I began in 2002 to produce and send out devotionals on the Internet. The first was *The Faith Files (*three volumes now available in print or online). Then I began a four-verse-per-day study from the New Testament. I kept doing those verse-by-verse studies for nine years, until I had completed the entire New Testament - all 8,000 verses! From there I went on to compile a short version of *A Daily Dose* called *A Daily Taste of Proverbs* and then *What Would Jesus Ask You Today?* - a devotional of questions asked in Scripture.

That brings me to this project that you have in your hand (or on your e-reader). I have taught on the topic of life purpose since 1991, and folded that concept of purpose into what I called "The Five Gold Mine Principles," which include purpose, goal setting, time management, organization and faith. I was teaching once on the Principles and someone responded to something I said with, "Oh, that's a pearl worth keeping." That got me thinking that I could write a daily devotional on the five Gold Mine Principles and call them pearls of wisdom. Once done, I could 'string' them together for what I would call *A String of Pearls*.

When I think of a pearl, it is something harvested from the sea. They are formed in an oyster as a grain of sand in the oyster creates an irritant, and the oyster relieves the discomfort by creating a pearl. There are pearls of different sizes and values, and there are pearls even come in a variety of colors. Divers can retrieve the pearls from great depths, which is why pearls are so costly

- they are rare and not easily gathered. Today, scientists can cultivate pearls through sophisticated techniques, but the oysters implanted with the irritant that will create the pearl are always returned to the sea for the pearl to develop.

What you have in this work is 366 days of pearls that you can apply to become more purposeful and creative. Since there are 12 months and five Gold Mine Principles, I had to do some maneuvering to make this work. Here is what I decided. I start in January with purpose, and then moved on to the other four principles in the months following. In June, I revisited purpose and in subsequent months went through the other four for a second time - all with different verses and content. Then in November, I produced a month's worth of Pearls on purpose (so there are three months on purpose) and finally in December I did a grab bag approach, harvesting pearls from all five Principles.

In this particular devotional, I started out with the title, then a passage of Scripture, and included a short body of reflective material. As is my custom, I put questions (in bold) in the content to help you apply what you read. For this particular devotional, I closed each one with a short italicized prayer. The purpose behind it all (I just can't get away from purpose) is to produce a short devotional you can read and apply quickly, but something that will be of value to you for a long period time - just like a pearl.

It is interesting that a 'pearl of wisdom' in our Western culture can actually be facetious for something nonsensical. That is not my intent as I use the phrase here. What I am trying to convey is that these daily devotions are pearls of wisdom that you can treasure and value as something from God's word that will help you embrace and engage His will for your life. If you string them together - applying all five Principles to your life - you will be more productive, joyful and healthy. As you 'wear' these Pearls, others will comment on the differences they see in you, just as if you were wearing a beautiful pearl necklace, earrings, bracelet or cuff links. And while pearls are more for women than men, obviously these pearls are of value for both men and women, and can adorn and beautify the life of any of God's servants.

I hope you will wear this *String of Pearls* for all to see and that you make the string bigger and bigger as you find those of value and add them to your life. As for me, however, it's time to move on and develop my next daily devotional, so I will present to you with this gift of Pearls so I can continue to work on my own application of the five Gold Mine Principles.

John W. Stanko
Pittsburgh, PA
June, 2014

January

Gold Mine Principle 1

Purpose

January 1
Stop Doing

"In those days when the number of disciples was increasing, the Hellenistic Jews among them complained against the Hebraic Jews because their widows were being overlooked in the daily distribution of food" - Acts 6:1.

Whenever you have personal or organizational growth, it presents new opportunities and problems. Your job will be to evaluate your 'world' to see what you can stop doing, what you can delegate and what you should keep on doing. That can be a difficult task, but it is critical for your ongoing effectiveness. **As you start a New Year, are you spread too thin? What can you stop doing so you can start doing more of what you do best?** *Lord, help me to know what to stop doing and give me the courage to actually stop!*

January 2
Your Yes

"So the Twelve gathered all the disciples together and said, 'It would not be right for us to neglect the ministry of the word of God in order to wait on tables'" - Acts 6:2.

The apostles were able to say 'no' to this request for help because they knew what the 'yes' was, which of course was their purpose. And because they knew their yes, they knew it would be 'wrong' to get involved, even though helping the widows was important work. **Are there good, or even noble, activities that are wrong for you? Do you know what you should say 'no' to because you know what your 'yes' is? Can you say** 'no' without feeling guilty? *Lord, I need your light and insight to understand what my purpose is. Then I need the courage to say 'no' to requests to do things not connected to my purpose, just like the apostles did.*

January 3
Trust Others

"Brothers and sisters, choose seven men from among you who are known to be full of the Spirit and wisdom. We will turn this responsibility over to them and will give our attention to prayer and the ministry of the word" - Acts 6:3-4.

When you let go of doing things you are emotionally attached to, you have to find and trust others who will have the same commitment as you. Therefore, you don't stop doing things by giving them to just anyone, but you still must find a way to stop doing them nonetheless. **Do you struggle with letting go? Is change difficult for you? Have you worked to train others so that they will carry tasks out with your same high standards (even your children)?** *Lord, my lack of trust in others is really a lack of trust in You. If You equipped me to do things, You can equip others to do them just as well or better. I release my roles and responsibilities to You, so I can embrace the new things You have for me. Help me to trust You and others!*

January 4
Focus

"We will turn this responsibility over to them and will give our attention to prayer and the ministry of the word" - Acts 6:4.

The goal in delegating is to have others do what they can do well so you can focus on what only you can do well. When the apostles prayed, buildings shook. When they ministered the Word, many came to know Jesus. **What is it that you do that 'shakes buildings?' Is it art? Listening? Fixing broken things? Healing the sick?** Whatever it is, stop doing whatever you can in order to invest more time in your purpose, gifts and goals. *Lord, I don't see how I can stop doing some things to more effectively do the things I love and am anointed to do. Help me to see my world as You see it, realizing that if I died today, someone would have to start doing what I do. How can I have that kind of urgency surrounding my purpose while yet living?*

January 5
Names

"This proposal pleased the whole group. They chose Stephen, a man full of faith and of the Holy Spirit; also Philip, Procorus, Nicanor, Timon, Parmenas, and Nicolas from Antioch, a convert to Judaism" - Acts 6:5.

To discover purpose, you must be a good listener, listening both to your heart and what others say. That starts by paying attention to other people's names when you meet them. It starts by *wanting* to know their name and then making an effort to pronounce and use it correctly. **How good are you at remembering names? What can you do to be more effective?** Give some thought to the role names can play in your PurposeQuest and then make a commitment to start listening to others more effectively, starting with their names. *Lord, my mind gets busy and preoccupied and that means I miss purpose, clues and signals that are* *coming my way. Help me to deal with my mind's clutter, and help me discipline myself to be a better listener, especially to pay better attention to others, which starts with acknowledging and remembering their names.*

January 6
Staying Close

"They presented these men to the apostles, who prayed and laid their hands on them" - Acts 6:6.

The apostles accepted the nominations from the people of those designated to help the widows. Not only did they accept them, but they also identified with them by laying hands on and praying for them. While the apostles could not get involved themselves, they did not totally ignore the situation, and prayed for the success of those who were elected. **Are you praying for the success of others in their purpose? Are you staying close to those to whom you have delegated duties?** That would mean first that you know what their purpose is and second, that you care enough to stay close in case they need help. *Lord, You instruct me to serve others and put their interests ahead of my own. Give me sensitivity to the duties and needs of others as they carry out their purpose and show me ways I can help them without taking back responsibilities I have turned over to them.*

January 7
Fruit

"So the word of God spread. The number of disciples in Jerusalem increased rapidly, and a large number of priests became obedient to the faith"
- Acts 6:7.

God's ways are effective. He may put you through a season of training where you don't see results, but that is the exception and not the rule. He wants you to fulfill your purpose more than you do, and will partner with you so that you have some measure of success in what it is He created you to do. **Are you happy with the fruit of purpose in your life? Are you afraid of or ambivalent about purpose results? Do you explain your lack of results away, saying it's not the will of God for you or the right season?** Part of your lack may be that you are engaged in good activities but not the correct ones for you to see results. *Lord, You desire for all Your disciples to bear fruit that will remain. I am Your disciple, so You expect fruit from my efforts. I will no longer be happy with trying hard alone, nor will I spin my lack of results to make me feel good when the fruit isn't there.*

January 8
Clarity

"In Joppa there was a disciple named Tabitha (in Greek her name is Dorcas); she was always doing good and helping the poor" - Acts 9:36.

This woman Dorcas had a personal purpose to care for the poor in a specific venue. Everyone else in the village saw the needs she saw, but only she was moved to action because God had created her to help the poor. Notice the clarity and simplicity of her purpose - just a few words that described what she best did most often. **Do you have this kind of clarity? Do you make your PurposeQuest too complicated? Are you actually so close to your situation that you cannot be objective? Do you need someone to help clarify your purpose?** *Lord, I have a purpose and it's simple and been with me all my life. Help me to see and to describe it with a few* words that explode with meaning, just like they did for Dorcas. Help me also to move past my wrong thinking that may cloud my perspective of who I am in Your eyes.

January 9
Evidence

"Peter went with them, and when he arrived he was taken upstairs to the room. All the widows stood around him, crying and showing him the robes and other clothing that Dorcas had made while she was still with them" - Acts 9:39.

When Peter arrived on the scene, the evidence of Tabitha's life purpose interceded on her behalf! The widows missed her, and they showed Peter all the garments she had made for them while she was alive. Tabitha didn't just talk about what she was going to do; she did it. If she was alive today, she would have a sewing machine and a source of cheap material and would be sewing for the poor, day and night. **Do you talk about what you are going to do 'one day'? Are you pursuing your purpose, whether or not you can make any money from it? What more can you do than you are doing now?** Lord, I am a good talker but not always a good doer. I am scared and don't know how to start. I have started but don't know how to finish. Help me, Lord, to find strategies that will enable me to assemble a body of purpose evidence that will represent me before You, even in my day of trouble.

January 10
Heaven's Resources

"Peter sent them all out of the room; then he got down on his knees and prayed. Turning toward the

dead woman, he said, 'Tabitha, get up.' She opened her eyes, and seeing Peter she sat up" - Acts 9:40.

In this story, it is easy to put the focus on Peter, for God used him to perform a great miracle. Let's look at it from Tabitha's perspective. Here was a 'nothing' woman ministering to 'nobody' people in a 'nowhere' town, but in her day of trouble, when she could not cry out for herself, the evidence of a life yielded to God's purpose cried out for her. And the most significant spiritual leader in the world at that time came to her rescue! When you are functioning in purpose, all the resources of heaven are at your disposal. **Are you praying like that is so? What do you need to make your purpose more effective? Why not pray for that today?** *Lord, at times I am guilty of asking for too little, acting like I will deplete your supply of something if I ask for too much. Yet You have something for me to do and I need Your help and provision to do it. I ask You for the resources to do Your will and I thank You in advance for Your provision.*

January 11
A Revival

"This became known all over Joppa, and many people believed in the Lord" - Acts 9:42.

Tabitha helped start a spiritual revival in her town, not because she was an evangelist, but because she was committed to helping the poor. When she died and Peter brought her back to life, her notoriety increased and people took notice of what God had done for her. This caused them to have faith in Christ for themselves. **Is your purpose commitment such that others notice? Do you preach the gospel, so to speak, without using words? Are you impacting the world through**

the fruit of your labors? *Lord, I come in contact with people every day. I pray I will shine for you by fulfilling my purpose. Help me to impact others' lives so that they will have to take notice and realize that it is You directing and energizing me. And let my daily witness help lead others to the same faith in You that I have.*

January 12
Light

"So then, King Agrippa, I was not disobedient to the vision from heaven" - Acts 26:19.

Paul found his purpose on the Damascus Road and called it 'vision from heaven.' The light he received that day was brighter than the noonday sun in the Middle East. That is the kind of intense and focused light God can shine on His will for your life. What's more, Paul stated that he was 'not disobedient' to that heavenly vision, which indicates that you can ignore or disobey God's purpose for your life. Paul chose not to do so. **What light has God given you concerning His will for your life? Are you stalling or putting off embracing that will?** *Lord, I accept Your will for my life. I will not run or delay, but will do what Paul did: accept Your will and partner with You to fulfill it. I put my trust in You for finances, wisdom and power to be effective and efficient in my own personal 'vision from heaven.'*

January 13
Compliments

"'Get up,' the Lord said, 'and go into Damascus. There you will be told all that you have been assigned to do'" - Acts 22:10.

Paul had an assignment and God took him to a place where people would let him know what that assignment was. God wants you to know your purpose and often sends people to provide clues and specific direction where your purpose is concerned. That often comes in the form of feedback and compliments, which you can easily ignore or misread. **Is there any compliment have you heard regularly that may be a key to your purpose? Why not ask some others to share with you what they see to be your strengths that may indicate purpose?** *Lord, I am open to hear what my purpose is from others, who may not have the bias I have toward who I am. Show me who I can ask and then give them Your insight that will help me know and do Your will for my life. Also show me anything others have regularly told me that is an indication of my purpose.*

January 14
Your Future

"When I returned to Jerusalem and was praying at the temple, I fell into a trance and saw the Lord speaking to me. 'Quick!' he said. 'Leave Jerusalem immediately, because the people here will not accept your testimony about me'" - Acts 22:17-18.

God understands your purpose and knows how people will respond. Here He directed Paul to leave his beloved Jews to go to the Gentiles, because the Lord knew the Jews would not accept Paul's testimony. God not only assigns your purpose but also becomes your purpose coach, directing your steps and development along the way. **Are you cooperating with God's plan, which may include school, being coached and trained, and travel? Are you trying to choose where you will be effective, or surrendering to where you will get the**

greatest results? *Lord, You know best because You see the future and can direct my steps to make sure I am ready to meet the challenges of tomorrow. I accept Your guidance and wisdom and will not fight what I must do to be successful in my purpose.*

January 15
Father Knows Best

"'Lord,' I replied, 'these people know that I went from one synagogue to another to imprison and beat those who believe in you'" - Acts 22:19.

When the Lord told Paul to leave Jerusalem, Paul objected, reasoning with the Lord that it made more sense for him to stay. Paul thought the people would recognize his conversion and repentance and accept his testimony. In other words, Paul wanted to choose his own purpose. The Lord made it easy, however, for Paul could either leave or die at the hands of his countrymen. **Are you resisting your purpose, holding out for what you want to do?** If so, then you are missing some of the abundant life that can be yours, and you need to surrender to God's plan if you want purpose success. *Lord, there are times when I felt I knew better than You what my purpose should be and where it should be expressed. I ask Your forgiveness for trying to run my life and I surrender today to Your purpose and plan. I will go where You want me to go and do what You want me to do. Show me what that is.*

January 16
Sphere of Influence

"Then the Lord said to me, 'Go; I will send you far away to the Gentiles'" - Acts 22:21.

You cannot say, "God, I will do whatever You want as long as it is in this country, in this city, on this street, with these people, in this building and on these days." God assigns not only your purpose but also your sphere of influence where and among whom your purpose will flourish and be most productive. **Do you know your sphere of influence? Among what group or in what setting are you most effective? Are you functioning in it? If not, why not? Of what are you afraid?** *Lord, I have an idea of where I am most effective, but I am dragging my feet. I am scared and I don't know how that will work out with my current responsibilities and duties. Help me to accept my sphere of influence and give me strategies to carry out my duties there.*

January 17
God's Call

"And the Lord said to Moses, 'See, I have called by name Bezalel son of Uri, the son of Hur, of the tribe of Judah'" - Exodus 31:1-2 (AMP).

When you are 'called,' it means God has spoken your name and you will 'hear' something that is meant only for you. Purpose is a message from your heavenly headquarters with your name on it. God had you specifically in mind for the job and no one can fulfill it as you can. What's more, God will speak your purpose to others so they know what it is and help open doors for you. **Do you have a sense of calling in your daily work? If not, what is the voice of God calling you to do? How can you expect your purpose to be clear to others if it's not clear to you?** *Lord, I want this sense of calling in my daily work. I will no longer be content just to be part of a group, but crave a sense of individual purpose in my life. I trust that You will speak clearly to* me, for my heart is tuned to hear You call my name regarding purpose. Speak, Lord, for Your servant listens!

January 18
Second-Nature

"And I have filled him with the Spirit of God, with wisdom, with understanding, with knowledge and with all kinds of skills" - Exodus 31:3.

The Lord filled Bezalel with 'all kinds of skills' and the same is probably true for you. These skills can be so natural for you, causing you to look past them as you search for purpose. What's more, they can seem rather 'unspiritual' as you consider that you do things like listen, teach, play with children, organize household items or remember names quite well. Yet all those things have been deposited in you by God's Spirit, so they all mean something as you seek to clarify your purpose. **Why not make a list today of all the skills you have, no matter how basic? Perhaps you can employ the help of others as you do?** *Lord, it is difficult for me to 'see' myself, but I want to recognize and acknowledge all the good skills with which You have filled me by Your Spirit. Show me who I am today. Don't let me look past those things that seem simple or second-nature to me, for you put them there for a reason.*

January 19
Handiwork

". . . to make artistic designs for work in gold, silver and bronze, to cut and set stones, to work in wood, and to engage in all kinds of crafts"
- Exodus 31:4-5.

God filled Bezalel with His Spirit, not to perform church duties like preaching, teaching or counseling. He filled him so he could work with his hands to create crafts. Bezalel's purpose was to work in his shop to produce works of art for the Lord! **Did you ever consider that your artistic abilities are more than just a family trait or personal interest, that they are initiated and supported by God's Spirit? When you crochet, paint, make jewelry or sew, do you see yourself performing 'spiritual' activities? Maybe it's time to consider your artistic endeavors to be more than a hobby or side interest?** *Lord, there are times when I have not considered my artistic talents to be special, let alone inspired by You. I accept these talents as gifts to me and the world around me. I ask for help to make them all they can be so I can do Your work and fulfill my purpose.*

January 20
Helpers

"Moreover, I have appointed Oholiab son of Ahisamak, of the tribe of Dan, to help him. Also I have given ability to all the skilled workers to make everything I have commanded you" - Exodus 31:6.

God did not make you capable of doing everything. When you know your purpose, you realize your need to be part of a team. That way you can do what only you can do and others can do the same. **Who are your team members? Which team are you a part of? What do you bring to the team? What do others bring?** *Lord, I am coming to realize my limitations as well as my strengths. I see that I need to be in a team in most everything I do, even though working with others can be difficult and even painful. Show me how I can be a contributing member of an effective team.*

January 21
God's Eyes

"They are to make them just as I commanded you" - Exodus 31:11.

The craftsmen, who were filled with God's Spirit to perform their duties, made the things for the tabernacle as the Lord directed them through Moses. God directed their purpose through their leader. What's more, some of what they made was seen by all and some was seen only by the high priest and God Himself! Your purpose may be public or it may be something you do for God's eyes only. **What has God filled you with His purpose to do? Who helps direct your purpose? Is your purpose more public or private?** *Lord, my purpose is from You, but You may use others to direct my purpose expressions. You may also have me do things that most people don't see or notice, but I know You notice them. I accept these limitations and commit to give my all no matter what, even if my work is seen by Your eyes only.*

January 22
What, Not How

"Moses thought that his own people would realize that God was using him to rescue them, but they did not" - Acts 7:25.

According to Stephen, Moses knew his purpose was to rescue the Jews who were in Egypt. Moses assumed everyone else knew that too, but they did not. So first Moses killed an Egyptian and hid the body. Then he tried to counsel his people to stop fighting with one another. Moses knew *what* he was supposed to do with his life, but he did not understand *how* he was to do it. This led him to do things that were not consistent with how he would ultimately rescue his people in God's power. **Do you know what you are supposed to do? Are you taking your time to prepare yourself and see the strategy for how you will do it?** This waiting on the strategy should not be passive, however, but is a time of spiritual and practical preparation. *Lord, I don't want to wait to fulfill my purpose, but I need you to show me **how** to prepare and **how** to do it. I don't want to sit, but I don't want to step out like Moses and do wrong things. Help me know **how** to do **what** it is You want me to do and I promise I will aggressively pursue it.*

January 23
Floating on Purpose

"At that time Moses was born, and he was no ordinary child. For three months he was cared for by his family" - Acts 7:20.

All newborns look pretty much alike, but Moses' parents saw something in their baby boy that was different. What did they see? They saw purpose! While all the other baby boys were being thrown into the river, they kept theirs for as long as they could. Then they complied with the edict, the only difference being they first put him in a floating basket. From there, Moses' purpose kept him safe and directed him into Pharaoh's household.

If you have children in your family or work with kids, what do you see? Do you see the problems or the potential? Have you released those children to God's will and purpose instead of your own? *Lord, I thank You for the children in my life. At times, I tend to look at their weaknesses and not their purpose. Help me to see that clearly and then help me know what I can do to encourage and develop that potential. Finally, give me* grace to release them so they can float on their purpose like Moses did on his.

January 24
Purposeful Teams

"On the contrary, they recognized that I had been entrusted with the task of preaching the gospel to the uncircumcised, just as Peter had been to the circumcised" - Galatians 2:7.

It is important you know your purpose so you can tell others what you do best. It's just as important to know the purpose of others, so you can know where their shoulders are broadest, so to speak, and where you can rely on them the most. Paul knew Peter's purpose. Peter knew Paul's. The other apostles knew Peter's and Paul's. That is why the early church grew, for everyone functioned in their purpose and gifts as God empowered them to be successful. **Do you know your purpose? Can you describe it to those with whom you work, live, and/or minister?** *Lord, I need clarity of purpose so I can know what I have to offer my family, team and church. I need the same clarity to know the purpose of my spouse, children, co-workers and team members. Make every team I am part of a well-oiled machine that can do great things for You in the power of purpose.*

January 25
Reassurance

"One night the Lord spoke to Paul in a vision: 'Do not be afraid; keep on speaking, do not be silent'" - Acts 18:9.

Someone once said when the Lord tells you not to be

afraid, it's usually too late! It is hard to imagine Paul being afraid, but in this instance he was. The Lord appeared to him to reassure him that he was doing well and that God would protect him. Your purpose can be a fearful thing because it seems so big and because you don't know how you will achieve it. Don't expect God to reassure you, however, unless you are *doing* something about and with your purpose. **Are you afraid of your purpose? Of what specifically are you fearful? Are you expecting some encouragement when you are not really engaged in your purpose?** *Lord, I am afraid of many things: what others think, what I think, failure, success, poverty, and personal growth. I am not asking for another confirmation of what I am to do, but I am asking that You affirm and encourage me today and every day as I take steps of purpose.*

January 26
Encouragement

"Last night an angel of the God to whom I belong and whom I serve stood beside me and said, 'Do not be afraid, Paul. You must stand trial before Caesar; and God has graciously given you the lives of all who sail with you'" - Acts 27:23-24.

When all on the ship to Rome appeared lost, an angel appeared to Paul, reminding Him of God's promise that he would witness to Caesar. Paul in turn encouraged everyone else with the words with which God had encouraged him. When you are functioning in purpose, God will provide abundant grace that helps and encourages you. **Are you giving your all to your purpose? Or sitting on the sidelines in fear, hoping that God will do what only you can do for yourself, which is obey His will for your life?** *Lord, I need Your* encouragement but I know I can only receive it when I have earned it. And I earn it by obediently taking steps to complete the purpose assignment You have given me. Forgive me for waiting for You to do what You expect me to, which is act in purposeful faith and hope.

January 27
Looking for You

"For two whole years Paul stayed there in his own rented house and welcomed all who came to see him. He proclaimed the kingdom of God and taught about the Lord Jesus Christ—with all boldness and without hindrance!" **- Acts 28:30-31.**

After all Paul had been through and even though he was a chained prisoner in Rome, God was with him to fulfill his purpose. He did not have to go looking for people to whom he could preach; they came looking for him, right to his very home! What's more, tradition has it that Paul led every one of his Roman guards to Jesus! That is the power of purpose; you don't have to go looking for it, it comes looking for you. **What group of people or activity always seem to find you, even in a crowd? What need presents itself to you regularly so you can provide the answer or cure?** Lord, I acknowledge that I have a purpose! Sometimes it is difficult to see because it is so second nature to me. Help me recognize what always seems to find me, and help me make sense out of that to define my purpose. Once I see and say it, help me be bold to **do** it, just like Paul was in Rome.

January 28
Your Joy, Not Your Job

"There he met a Jew named Aquila, a native of

Pontus, who had recently come from Italy with his wife Priscilla, because Claudius had ordered all Jews to leave Rome. Paul went to see them, and because he was a tentmaker as they were, he stayed and worked with them" - Acts 18:2-3.

Paul wrote 13 letters, but never once told us what he did to make money. Yet in every letter he told us about his purpose, which was to take the gospel to the Gentiles. Paul did not take his identity from what he did to make money, but rather from what he did that gave him the greatest fulfillment. You may or may not make money from your purpose, but it is the main reason you are here and alive. **Have you been defining yourself by your occupation instead of purpose? If you are frustrated with your job, what can you do after work that is purpose-related?** *Lord, I thank You for Your provision, but often my work is not a good expression of who I am. Yet my culture urges me to define myself by what I do for a living. Help me be free from this thinking and to see my purpose in a new light so I can describe myself to others and myself by my joy and not my job.*

January 29
A Different Perspective

"Our dear friend Luke, the doctor, and Demas send greetings" - Colossians 4:14.

Luke reported what Paul did to make money in Acts and Paul returned the favor by telling us what Luke did in Colossians. Neither man introduced or identified himself by what he did to earn a living, but by what he did that gave him joy and expressed purpose. If you love missions but sell insurance, for example, perhaps you should follow Paul and Luke's example and introduce yourself as a missionary, even if you only go abroad for two weeks a year. **How do you see yourself where money, occupation and purpose are concerned? What identity is uppermost in your mind? Do you need a change of thinking and perspective on this matter?** *Lord, if I keep on doing and thinking as I always have, I will continue to get the same results. I need to see my life, work and world differently and I need help to do so. Help me see myself from a purpose perspective and give me the courage to state that to the world, not fearing criticism or ridicule.*

January 30
Divine Energy

"I became a servant of this gospel by the gift of God's grace given me through the working of his power" - Ephesians 3:7.

The word for power here is derived from the Greek 'energeo,' from which the English word 'energy' comes. Your purpose is a gift and it comes through a divine working of His power in you. It also energizes you, so much so that you can lose sleep and not eat while functioning in purpose and still be effective, enthusiastic and joyful. **What are you energized to do? When do you sense God's energy flowing with and through you?** *Lord, I thank You for my purpose, whether or not I can see what it is. I also thank You for Your divine energy and power that works through me in purpose, even if I am not clear what that purpose is. I trust You will show me purpose and also help me see where Your energy flows most abundantly in my life.*

January 31
Life Patterns

"Jacob's well was there, and Jesus, tired as he was from the journey, sat down by the well. It was about noon. When a Samaritan woman came to draw water, Jesus said to her, 'Will you give me a drink?'"
- John 4:6-7.

Jesus sat down to rest and wait for lunch, but the Father had other ideas and brought a needy woman to Him. You seldom have to go looking for purpose, it almost always comes looking for you. God wants you to fulfill your purpose more than you do and that's why He brings opportunities, people and situations across your path. **Think about your life as far back as possible and see what situation has repeatedly sought you out to be involved? What scenario or problem always finds you because you can help or have some answers?** *Lord, I know You are not trying to trick me by bringing things into my life to test whether or not I will or will not engage them. Help me to see any life patterns of things that always seem to find me to be involved because You want me involved. Help me not to miss anything so I can recognize my purpose.*

February

Gold Mine Principle 2

Goals

February 1
Obstacles

"I press on toward the goal to win the prize for which God has called me heavenward in Christ Jesus"
- Philippians 3:14.

Paul pressed on. That meant something was already pressing against him, and he needed to exert more force to make progress. What did Paul use to motivate him to press on? He used a goal! You also need goals to press on through the fear, ignorance, laziness and pessimism that can all too easily debilitate you. **What is pressing against you to keep you where you currently are? What goals are helping you press on through the barriers?** *Lord, I admit that many things press against me to keep me average, mediocre and in the status quo. I need to harness what you put in my heart to do, and can only do that by having goals. Help me clarify and establish goals that will help me make progress in You.*

February 2
The Prize

"I press on toward the goal to win the prize for which God has called me heavenward in Christ Jesus"
- Philippians 3:14.

Paul wanted to win the prize. Goals speak of winners and losers. If you set the goal, you may not make it. If you don't set the goal, you definitely won't make it. Where goal setting is concerned, however, it is better to be sorry for trying than safe for not, for the joys of achieving a goal are far greater than any regret of failure. **What prize are you seeking in life? Are you so afraid of losing that you don't even try to win the**

prize? Are you afraid to admit that to yourself?
Lord, I want to achieve, but sometimes I am so afraid of losing that I don't even try, or talk myself out of it. Then at other times I am not sure it's consistent with Your will to achieve the prize and I get bogged down in doubt. Help me, Lord, with my fears and confusion, and then help me focus on the prize of the goals in my heart!

February 3
God's Thoughts

"I press on toward the goal to win the prize for which God has called me heavenward in Christ Jesus"
- Philippians 3:14.

Paul saw his goal as something God called him to do. You can think of your goals as the same. Proverbs 16:3 states in the Amplified Version: "Roll your works upon the Lord [commit and trust them wholly to Him; He will cause your thoughts to become agreeable to His will, and] so shall your plans be established *and* succeed." God wants you to know His will, so your thoughts can be God's if you commit your way to Him. Then you simply translate those thoughts into goals. **What has God put in your heart that seems like a calling? Have you converted that into an action goal? If not, why not do it now?** *Lord, I trust you are not leading me astray. I want to know Your will and find ways to do it. As I commit my way to Your will, I know You are guiding my thoughts to be Your thoughts. Help me set goals with confidence that You are leading and guiding the entire process.*

February 4
Godly Goals

"I press on toward the goal to win the prize for which

God has called me heavenward in Christ Jesus"
- Philippians 3:14.

Paul's goals brought him heavenward, or closer to God and godliness. His goals helped him become more Christ-like. Paul knew he was in Christ, so his goals were part and parcel with his service to God and His people. **Do you have godly goals? Have you set goals concerning God's word, giving, service and spiritual growth? Do you always write down your goals to keep them before you, so you don't lose momentum or forget?** *Lord, I want to do more than merely exist, only taking up space and resources. I want to be productive for You. At the same time, I want what I do to make me more like You as I pursue my goals in faith. May my goals all take me heavenward as I do Your will on a daily basis.*

February 5
Clarity

"My goal is that they may be encouraged in heart and united in love, so that they may have the full riches of complete understanding, in order that they may know the mystery of God, namely, Christ"
- Colossians 2:2.

Paul did not teach just to take up time or hear himself talk. He had goals in mind when he taught and asked himself what he wanted his teaching to produce in those who heard. That led to purposeful teaching and tremendous results, both in his teaching and writing. **What goals and objectives do you have in mind? What are you hoping or trying to produce? Is it clear?** If it's not clear to you, then it won't be clear to others and you will be frustrated with meager results.

Lord, I want to have purpose in what I do, and I see that having goals will help me have that. Yet sometimes it's difficult to identify what I am trying to accomplish, which often leads me to put off setting a goal and I consequently do nothing. Help me be clear about what I am doing in my activities of life.

February 6
Faith

"So we make it our goal to please him, whether we are at home in the body or away from it" - 2 Corinthians 5:9.

There is only one way to please God and that is to have faith. Your goals should involve faith, which means you don't have to know all the answers beforehand. That should free you to set substantial goals that will require you to grow and learn in order to achieve them. Mostly, however, those faith-stretching goals will bring you closer to God. **Do you have faith goals? Goals that you have no idea how you will accomplish? Is it your goal to please God in this process? Do you see goals as spiritual or worldly?** *Lord, I want to exercise faith that pleases You, so if goals can help do that, I want to set them more than ever! Deliver me from having to know it all before I take the first steps of formulating my goals. I know that you can do the impossible, but I am not always convinced You can and will for me, so help my unbelief!*

February 7
Scripture

"At the present time your plenty will supply what they need, so that in turn their plenty will supply

what you need. The goal is equality, as it is written: 'The one who gathered much did not have too much, and the one who gathered little did not have too little'" - 2 Corinthians 8:14-15.

Paul derived his life's values from Scripture and set his goals accordingly. In these verses, we see he had a goal for a special relief fund collection, and that goal was equality so that no one had too much or too little. Paul had an objective in mind whenever he taught or wrote, and you would do well to follow his example. **Is Scripture influencing and determining your goals? How can your goals be more Bible-based? Do you have purpose in what you do and is that purpose helping you set goals to see your purpose achieved?** *Lord, I know your Word is a lamp unto my feet, so help me see Your word in a whole new way. I want to set goals that are pleasing to you, goals that emanate from a study of and commitment to Your word. Help me to be more purposeful in all I do, for I know success in You is never an accident.*

February 8
Duty vs. Joy

"For the joy set before him he endured the cross, scorning its shame, and sat down at the right hand of the throne of God" - Hebrews 12:2.

You accomplish goals not because you have to, but because you choose to do so. And if the joy of the end result is not uppermost in your mind and ever before you, you will lose heart and hope along the way. Jesus kept the joy of the goal before Him and that enabled Him to endure the cross and despise the shame. You will do well to emulate His example. **Are your goals joyful or**

duty-bound? Is the vision of the end result so clear in your mind that you will endure whatever you must to see that vision come to pass? *Lord, joy was Your motivator and I want it to be mine as well. But my fears and concept of what I think it means to serve You cause me at times to abandon joy and embrace duty. I want to set goals that stem from my joy so that I can have Your strength to endure and achieve.*

February 9
Be Aggressive

"It has always been my ambition to preach the gospel where Christ was not known, so that I would not be building on someone else's foundation. Rather, as it is written: 'Those who were not told about him will see, and those who have not heard will understand'" - Romans 15:20-21.

Substitute the word 'purpose' for ambition above and you will see that Paul had ministry goals, which is why in part he was so successful. While led by the Spirit, Paul was always looking and planning ahead as to how he could be more effective. Also, Paul had values that determined his ambitious actions, and we see his value in this verse was not to build on another's foundation. **Do you see goals as spiritual? Are you aggressively pursuing your goals? Have you spelled out your values that will help you set goals and ultimately fulfill your purpose?** *Lord, I realize that achieving things for You cannot be passive. Once I have my purpose, I need to identify values and set goals that will help me be fruitful. I confess that I have not always seen ambition as godly, but I see I must be ambitious for Your will and purpose, and goals will help me do so.*

February 10
Set Some Goals

"But now that there is no more place for me to work in these regions, and since I have been longing for many years to visit you, I plan to do so when I go to Spain. I hope to see you while passing through and to have you assist me on my journey there, after I have enjoyed your company for a while"
- Romans 15:23-24.

Paul laid plans to visit Rome. That's another way of saying that he had a goal to go there. Some believe that planning is ungodly and unspiritual, but as long as the Lord has the last say and you know your goal-setting is not perfect, you will do well to set as many goals in your life as possible. Sit down today and work on some spiritual, financial, family, educational, and health goals. What have you got to lose? If goals are not godly, then you won't achieve them. If they are, then you will release tremendous energy and potential when you set those goals. **What holds you back from setting goals? Do you see that Paul had goals? Then why aren't you also?** *Lord, I am learning that goals will help me achieve more for and in You. Yet I am naturally hesitant to set them. Show me why I am like that, and help me change.*

February 11
Mental Notes

"I will stand at my watch and station myself on the ramparts; I will look to see what he will say to me, and what answer I am to give to this complaint. Then the Lord replied: 'Write down the revelation and make it plain on tablets so that a herald may run with it. For the revelation awaits an appointed time;

it speaks of the end and will not prove false. Though it linger, wait for it; it will certainly come and will not delay'" - Habbakuk 2:1-3.

Yesterday you were urged to write goals. How can you do this? You will do it just as God directed the prophet. You will sit, listen and write them plainly. Someone once said the problem with taking mental notes is that the ink fades so quickly. So you must write down what it is you have set your mind and heart to do. Don't worry about whether they are right or wrong at this point, or they are written correctly. Trust that God is leading you and write them down. **What is stopping you from sitting down and writing out goals? Why not set a time to write them today, allowing at least two hours?** Don't talk yourself out of it! Keep focused on the things you feel led to do, which God will help you achieve. *Lord, I trust You are leading me, so I will sit down to listen and write some goals. Guide my mind and steps to do Your will and then give me the courage and strength to follow through. I want to be focused and diligent but I need Your help!*

February 12
No Shortcuts

"The plans of the diligent lead to profit as surely as haste leads to poverty" - Proverbs 21:5.

Part of any planning by diligent people involves setting goals, including such common areas of life as financial planning for retirement, job promotions or exercise. There are no shortcuts to success and winning the lottery is a remote possibility for those looking for a shortcut around goals. Once the goal is set, diligence is required to stay the course and finish the task. **Do you have goals for every area of life? Are you diligent to** follow through on the hard work and commitment it takes to reach that goal? *Lord, I often look for easy ways to success and goal fulfillment, but there seldom is. First, I want to be a person of my word, and that includes promises to myself. Give me strength and vision to hold onto a goal when it looks bleak, and deliver me from a mindset that looks for shortcuts to success.*

February 13
Talk Is Easy

"All hard work brings a profit, but mere talk leads only to poverty" - Proverbs 14:23.

It is so easy to talk about what you will do 'one day.' Yet this is the day that the Lord has made and it is the only one you are guaranteed to have! It is critical that you move beyond talk to action. Goals will help you do that. **What have you talked about doing one day? How can you set it in a goal that give is a specific date by which it will be accomplished? Do you have a five-year or ten-year plan to guide your 'today'?** While you are not guaranteed tomorrow, you should act today like you will be here for a long time, and that will enable you to set and work toward long-term goals. *Lord, I realize my times are in Your hands. I must learn to work like I will be here for a long time, but with the urgency that I may not have much time left. Help me to move past glib talk to firm goals that will enable me to make the most of today and every day as I pursue Your will for my life.*

February 14
The Reward

"David had said, 'Whoever leads the attack on the Jebusites will become commander-in-chief.' Joab

son of Zeruiah went up first, and so he received the command" - 1 Chronicles 11:6.

David offered a reward to help him accomplish his goal of conquering Jerusalem. And Joab's personal goal was to lead, so his goal fit perfectly with David's goal. All goals offer a reward that you want, not that you feel you must achieve or else. And your group goals must include rewards for those participating. **Are you clear on the reward attached to your goals? Do you keep that reward uppermost in your mind during the goal-achieving process? Are you ambivalent about rewards and instead set goals that are joyless and duty-bound?** *Lord, You created me to work with purpose. You also created me with the desire to achieve and that achievement will bring joy and other rewards for completing the task. I refuse to feel guilty as I pursue my goal rewards, and I ask You to help me work with others to help them pursue and obtain the same.*

February 15
Financial Gain

"Lazy hands make for poverty, but diligent hands bring wealth" - Proverbs 10:4.

Often when you pray for money, God gives you an idea. When you translate that idea into reality, you will have the money for which you prayed. Part of turning that idea into financial gain is goal setting. **Is some of your current lack due to your lack of diligence to follow through to set and pursue your goals? Have you looked for some financial shortcut rather than doing the work that leads to true wealth and prosperity?** *Lord, I confess that I have looked for shortcuts and not been diligent to set and pursue my goals. I have fretted* over my lack of money, instead of my lack of diligence. Help me to see the potential in my ideas and help me to set goals to achieve them. Then help me be diligent through the challenges ahead.

February 16
Silly Hunter

"The lazy do not roast any game, but the diligent feed on the riches of the hunt"
- Proverbs 12:27.

Imagine a hunter going through all the trouble of hunting and finding game, only to leave the game lying on the ground once the hunt is completed. That is a silly image, but that is exactly what you do when you have an idea and don't attach a goal to it. What's more, the goal isn't the only benefit you achieve, but the pursuit of the goal brings with it untold opportunities for growth! **Are you like the silly hunter described in this proverb? Do you spout forth ideas and concepts, but do nothing to finish them, such as setting and pursuing a goal?** *Lord, I am at times like this silly hunter. I have not been diligent to feed on the growth opportunities You provide when I pursue my ideas and dreams. I don't want to leave valuables on the field any longer, but want to pursue and overtake my goals, feasting on their results and giving You glory in the process.*

February 17
Lazy

"A sluggard's appetite is never filled, but the desires of the diligent are fully satisfied"
- Proverbs 13:4.

When you are lazy, you can have all kinds of dreams, but they are never satisfied or fulfilled. Most of your laziness is rooted in fear - fear of not finishing, fear of finishing, fear of failure, fear of criticism. So if you are going to deal with your laziness, perhaps you need to start by facing your fears and why you choose to sit on the couch and watch television rather than write, study or serve. **Have you succumbed to laziness? What is the source of your laziness? Apathy? Fear? Anxiety? Lack of personal development?** *Lord, at times there is no explanation for my inactivity except for laziness. I want to understand why I am lazy, for You certainly created me to work and achieve. When I am lazy, I am thwarting Your plans for my life. Reveal my heart and let me know why I have a tendency to inaction and then grant me grace to repent.*

February 18
Clarity

"He is the one we proclaim, admonishing and teaching everyone with all wisdom, so that we may present everyone fully mature in Christ. To this end I strenuously contend with all the energy Christ so powerfully works in me" - Colossians 1:28-29.

Paul had an end in mind when he taught. He wasn't just teaching but wanted to produce something in others, and worked toward that end. You should do the same with your goals. Be clear as to what you want to achieve. **Do you have your goal's end result clear in mind? Are you clear as to what you want to accomplish? Have you put it into words that are graphic and specific?** *Lord, I am sometimes afraid to be specific, for fear that I may not be able to make it. Yet I know if I am not clear where I am going, any road will do. I ask you to help* me focus and clarify the end results You put in my heart to achieve, and then to spell them out clearly, with no ambivalence or fear.

February 19
Your Land

"Those who work their land will have abundant food, but those who chase fantasies have no sense"
- Proverbs 12:11.

You have a land to work. It is not agricultural, but it may be in education, business, ministry or the military. Your goals will keep you 'grounded,' so to speak, and enable you to move beyond wishful and mere talk to achievement and productivity. **Do you know what your 'land' is? Are you setting goals in that area, trusting in God's help to accomplish them? Or do you have gigantic dreams that are so beyond your reach that you are just faking it and really pursuing or talking fantasies?** *Lord, there are times I have not worked my field or land You assigned to me. First, I thank You for my land, whether or not I fully see it today. I ask You to open my eyes so I can see it, and then give me strategies to work it so that there is abundant purposeful food for me and all those with whom I work.*

February 20
Faith Goals

"One day Jonathan son of Saul said to his young armor-bearer, 'Come, let's go over to the Philistine outpost on the other side'" - 1 Samuel 14:1.

Jonathan was hopelessly outnumbered when he decided one day to set a goal, and that was to attack the

Philistine garrison that had been plaguing his people. He had faith and was clear about what he wanted to do. Notice also that he impacted and involved others, well, at least his armor bearer, when he set the goal. **What impossible (for you) goals have you set? Must you have all the answers before you set the goal?** If you do, then it's not a goal, it's a forecast or prediction! *Lord, I have sung songs that spoke of Your ability to do the impossible, yet I have remained in my comfort zone, choosing to do nothing. You don't want Your power commemorated in song, however, but in my daily life! I want my life to count, and that will require me to have and use great faith. Help me, I pray!*

February 21
Confidentiality

"No one was aware that Jonathan had left"
- 1 Samuel 14:3.

When Jonathan decided to attempt his nearly impossible goal, he did not tell anyone, except for his sidekick the armor bearer. Why? His father's army gathered every day to do nothing by a pomegranate tree and perhaps Jonathan knew they would try to talk him out of the goal. The lesson is clear: Only share your goals with those you trust and who can help you achieve them. **Have you ever been discouraged by others as you set goals? Discouraged others yourself? Who do you know that you can trust in this process?** *Lord, the things You put in my heart are for me and may not be understood by others, even those closest to me. While I want the affirmation of others, I am ready to go it alone and rely on Your support and strength as I set and pursue goals. I do ask, however, that You send someone to encourage me along the way.*

February 22
Cliffs

"On each side of the pass that Jonathan intended to cross to reach the Philistine outpost was a cliff; one was called Bozez and the other Seneh"
- 1 Samuel 14: 4.

The cliffs Jonathan faced were so imposing that they were given names! That made them serious cliffs to climb and overcome. Yet the daunting task only became possible because he had set a goal and the cliffs just happened to be in his way. **Do you set the goal and then face the obstacles, or do you look at the obstacles and then decide whether or not to set the goal? Are the cliffs in your life keeping you from getting to the next level? What are you prepared to do about them?** *Lord, mountains are a part of life, but I allow them to intimidate and keep me from moving onward and upward. The highest mountain to me, however, is nothing to You. I need to live in Your perspective and not my own. With Your help, I determine to set goals regardless of the obstacles and trust You for the outcome.*

February 23
Perhaps

"Come, let's go over to the outpost of those uncircumcised men. Perhaps the Lord will act in our behalf. Nothing can hinder the Lord from saving, whether by many or by few" - 1 Samuel 14:6.

Jonathan had faith but he had imperfect understanding and information, so he said 'perhaps the Lord will act.' When you set a goal, the future lies ahead of you and you cannot see it clearly or perfectly. Therefore you set your goals in faith, but you realize that things can change or happen over which you have no control. **Are you waiting to have everything figured out and foreseen before you set a goal? Are you willing to fail while pursuing success? Are you willing to start over if you do fail?** *Lord, You control the future, I don't. Therefore I will function in what I know today, set a goal and trust You for the results tomorrow. If it doesn't work out, I still trust You and will learn from the experience so I can be more effective the next time. Give me the same attitude that Jonathan had when he decided to climb those cliffs!*

February 24
Heart Goals

"'Do all that you have in mind,' his armor-bearer said. 'Go ahead; I am with you heart and soul'"
- 1 Samuel 14:7.

Goals involve the mind and the heart. You should involve rational thought, but also heartfelt emotion and passion. Jonathan had someone who encouraged him to do what was in his heart and the armor bearer promised to support him. **What is in your heart to do? Why do you leave it in your heart? Why not draw it out by setting a goal? And do you have the support you need from those who can help? Are you in a position to help others with their heart goals?** *Lord, I get hung up sometimes, concerned whether or not what is in my heart is from You. Yet those things have been in my heart for a while and I am tired of my inactivity, putting things off until tomorrow. Send me those who can help me achieve goals and show me where I can help others achieve theirs.*

February 25
Confirmation

"Jonathan said, 'Come on, then; we will cross over toward them and let them see us. If they say to us, 'Wait there until we come to you,' we will stay where we are and not go up to them. But if they say, 'Come up to us,' we will climb up, because that will be our sign that the Lord has given them into our hands'"
- 1 Samuel 14:8-10.

Jonathan looked for confirmation before he set out on his goal, but it wasn't what you would think to ask for. He didn't ask for the sun to stop or five rocks to fall at his feet. He simply said if his enemies called him up to their high place, he would take that as a sign to go. He wasn't looking for an eccentric sign; He was looking for the simplest of confirmations in order to go. **What about you? Have you contrived a complex series of confirmations before you will take the first faith step toward your goal? Or are you looking for some small, little thing that will speak to you and enable you to go forth?** *Lord, I often look for reasons **not** to do what's in my heart instead of reasons to move forward. I do this because of fear. You have given me all the confirmation I need with the inner peace I feel when I consider my goal. Forgive my unbelief and give me encouragement today to help me get started.*

February 26
Your Effort

"Jonathan climbed up, using his hands and feet, with his armor-bearer right behind him. The Philistines fell before Jonathan, and his armor-bearer followed and killed behind him. In that first

> ***attack Jonathan and his armor-bearer killed some twenty men in an area of about half an acre"***
> ***- 1 Samuel 14:13-14.***

Jonathan and his companion had to scale two cliffs to reach their goal, cliffs that had names! That means they faced the risk of falling, had to get their fingernails dirty and probably scraped their arms and legs. The point is that they had to work hard to reach their destination. Once they did, God helped them and granted them great favor. Once they did what only they could do, God did what only He could do. **Are you waiting for God to do what only you can do? How much energy are you investing in your goals? What more do you need to do to succeed?** *Lord, I sometimes get confused between my role and Yours as I seek to do Your will. Help me understand when to wait on You and when to act like it's all up to me! I know You want to partner with me as I do Your will, and I want to do my part faithfully. Help me climb my cliffs and give me success to reach the top.*

February 27
Delay Tactic

> ***"Saul said to Ahijah, 'Bring the ark of God.' (At that time it was with the Israelites.) While Saul was talking to the priest, the tumult in the Philistine camp increased more and more. So Saul said to the priest, 'Withdraw your hand'" - 1 Samuel 14:18-19.***

While Jonathan was climbing and fighting, the army of God was on maneuvers and then asking for the ark so they could seek the Lord about His will. His will, however, was for them to fight and eventually they had to stop stalling and start acting. If you are going to pray about your goals, then do so actively and fervently. Don't use prayer, however, as a delay tactic, blaming your inactivity on the Lord and His refusal to respond. **What does your prayer life consist of where your goals are concerned? What are you hearing? Are you praying looking to act, or are you praying looking to wait?** *Lord, I confess that at times I have used prayer to delay acting on my goals. Then I have blamed You for my lack of effort, not really wanting to act, but using Your lack of response, or my lack of listening, as the reason for my inactivity. No longer will I use You as an excuse, but will pray and act or not pray at all.*

February 28
Testimony

"When all the Israelites who had hidden in the hill country of Ephraim heard that the Philistines were on the run, they joined the battle in hot pursuit"
- 1 Samuel 14:22.

When you pursue and achieve goals, you give others permission to do the same. While some may not notice, others will, and you will provide a reason for them to ask how you did it and then set off to set their own goals. While your goals are private, the process and results are not, for those become your testimony, and you give testimonies publicly to glorify God and encourage others. **How recent is your latest goal testimony? With whom have you shared it? What more can you do to stimulate others to 'good deeds' as the writer of Hebrews called it?** *Lord, I value my privacy but You don't. You want my life to be an encouragement and witness to others and that requires I be more public than I would prefer. Help me overcome my shyness and fear.*

Give me opportunities in which I can glorify You and stimulate the interest and activity of others toward goals.

February 29
Synergy

"So on that day the Lord saved Israel, and the battle moved on beyond Beth Aven" - 1 Samuel 14:23.

When Jonathan started out to climb his cliffs, he had no idea that his goal would affect so many people. He impacted his armor bearer, his father and the army, the people who had joined the Philistines and the people who were in hiding, not to mention the Philistines themselves, whom Israel routed in battle. Jonathan's goal created synergy and many people got involved to accomplish greater things than any of them could have done alone. **Do your goals have that kind of synergistic power? Are your goals large enough to impact others? Do you have faith that you can impact others?** *Lord, deliver me from my small little world of comfort and control. There is a needy world out there and I want to make my mark by helping others through my vision and faith. While I leave the scope and results of my goals to You, I pray that I would do my part and trust You to multiply my efforts for Your purposes.*

March

Gold Mine Principle 3

Time

March 1
24 Hours

*"Therefore be careful how you walk,
not as unwise men but as wise, making
the most of your time, because the days are evil"
- Ephesians 5:15-16.*

You have all the time in the world - 24 hours every day you are alive. You don't get more than that, so what you do with each day determines whether or not you are effective for the Lord or just putting in your time. **How often have you wasted an hour or two because you didn't have a plan on how to use them?** Then you may complain to others how busy you are with no time to do what you want or enjoy. **Are you making the most of your time? Are you aware of how much time you waste on frivolous activities, like silly television shows? Are you prepared this month to address time-wasting habits?** *Lord, I thank You for the gift of the 24 hours You have bestowed upon me today. I want to make the most of them. Help me this month to address this important issue and things in my life keeping me from effectively using the time You loan me. I want to do a better job than I have at this point in life.*

March 2
A Dull Axe

*"If the ax is dull and its edge unsharpened, more strength is needed, but skill will bring success"
- Ecclesiastes 10:10.*

It's not that you don't have the capability to manage your time, it's that you have never been trained. Today's verse points out that you can chop down a tree with a dull axe; it simply requires more effort and energy. When you sharpen the axe, however, the work is easier. It's the same with your time. You are going to gain skills this month to sharpen your axe and you will find you are doing more work with less stress and energy expended. **Do you recognize the need to be trained in time management skills? Do you want to be more proficient in this area? What will this skill do for and in your life?** *Lord, I need help in this area of my life and I look to You this month to give me new skills and tips that will help me be more productive with less stress and guilt! I want to sharpen my axe and work smarter and not harder; therefore I commit to apply myself to this area of life and increase my skill where time use is concerned.*

March 3
Times

*"There is a time for everything,
and a season for every activity under the heavens:
a time to be born and a time to die,
a time to plant and a time to uproot,
a time to kill and a time to heal,
a time to tear down and a time to build"
- Ecclesiastes 3:1-3.*

There is a time for everything, but this famous list of 'times' leads one to ask: **How do I know what time it is?** The activities listed are diametrically opposed to one another, and that is what you face every day. **Should I rest or work? Write a letter or watch a movie? Read or play with my children? Prepare for the future or write about the past?** You will look at the key to knowing what time it is tomorrow, but for today, spend some time reflecting on the seasons of your life past that may hold clues to what time or season you are in today.

Lord, there are so many things I can be doing. How can I know what it is that I should be doing? Do you set those times or do I help determine them by my choices and will? Show me what 'time' it is and help me to eliminate the other options and focus until its time is up!

March 4
Certainty

***"... from Issachar, men who understood the times and knew what Israel should do—200 chiefs, with all their relatives under their command"
- 1 Chronicles 12:32.***

Yesterday you were asked what time it is, asking if you know what you should be doing in this season and moment of life. It must be possible to know, as we see in today's verse. The men of this tribe presented themselves to King David, aware of what time it was and what they were supposed to do. **Do you have that kind of awareness? Do you want it? What have you wanted to do but have been unable to find time to do it?** Tomorrow you will learn a principle to help you be as certain as the sons of Issachar were in today's verse! In the meantime, search your heart to ensure you are ready for this kind of focus. *Lord, I have often stumbled around, guessing what I was supposed to be doing, sometimes waiting when I should act and acting when I should wait. I need the kind of certainty that I see in today's verse. Yet, that certainty brings the responsibility to act and that is a fearful thing for me. Help me, Lord!*

March 5
Veto Power

"Anyone who chooses to do the will of God will

find out whether my teaching comes from God or whether I speak on my own" - John 7:17.

People asked Jesus how they could know if His teaching was from God. Jesus' response was simple: If anyone wants to know, he or she will know. If you commit to do God's will *before* you know what it is, then God is obligated to reveal His will to you. That includes how you should invest your time and to what projects you should devote the precious minutes you have. **Have you surrendered your veto power over God's will *before* you know what His will is? Do you really trust and believe that God can reveal His will to you? Or, like many, do you believe He is tempting you with attractive options while trying to entrap you to make a bad decision?** *Lord, I surrender my right to veto Your will, and I do that **before** I know what it is! As I do that, I trust You to reveal Your will, including how I should invest the minutes and hours available to me every day. I want to do Your will, and am confident You will reveal it to me so that I will know, as Jesus promised.*

March 6
Sincerity

"Now that you know these things, you will be blessed if you do them" - John 13:17.

Yesterday you saw how to determine the will of God for your time, and that is to commit to do it *before* you know what it is. Once you know (and God will show you for sure), you are only blessed when you carry out God's plan, not when you talk about it or make sincere efforts in your mind to do something about it 'one day'. **What is it that you know you should do but are not doing? Where have you convinced yourself that, because** you are sincere, your sincerity can take the place of action and results?** *Lord, You have revealed Your will for my life and time. I have allowed fear and wrong thinking to blur and dilute that revelation, causing me to do little or nothing with what I know. Forgive me, Lord, for thinking my sincerity can substitute for obedience. I want the blessing of action and will pursue it today.*

March 7
Urgent Voices

"Put your outdoor work in order and get your fields ready; after that, build your house" - Proverbs 24:27.

Time management is not about getting more things done in less time. It is about the discipline and focus to get the most important things done in the midst of competing voices that are urgently crying out, "Pay attention to me!" Tomorrow you will start looking at a principle that will help you establish priorities in your life but, for now, you need to see the importance of priorities in your life as you manage time. **Are your priorities clearly set on a daily basis? Do you follow them or do you only talk about them? What urgent voices are vying for and winning your time?** *Lord, I am easily distracted, and that causes me to pay attention to things that don't matter, or matter less than the most important things and people in my life. I need help to focus and the discipline to stay there! Show me how to establish and keep priorities so I can keep the main thing the main thing every day.*

March 8
Basic Needs

"But seek first his kingdom and his righteousness,

and all these things will be given to you as well"
- Matthew 6:33.

Your natural tendency is to first seek the basic necessities of life. Jesus cautioned you not to make those your priority, but to seek God's will and rule in your life first and foremost. What does that mean? It means that prayer, reading, devotions and, above all, God's purpose, are to be your main focus. When you do that, God promises to provide for those basic needs. **Are you putting God's kingdom ahead of your own needs? Or are you consumed with the drive for promotion, salary and benefits? Are you trusting God for your basic needs or have you taken matters into your own hands?** *Lord, You promised to provide for me while I pursue Your will, and You have never broken Your word. Yet I am consumed at times with those things that pertain to life and career and forget to seek Your will first. I commit to seek Your kingdom and trust You for the rest, according to Your word and will for my life.*

March 9
Governing Values

"Every Sabbath he reasoned in the synagogue, trying to persuade Jews and Greeks" - Acts 18:4.

Every place Paul went, he first visited the synagogue to preach and proclaim Jesus. He did this not because Scripture commanded it but because he had a governing value that helped direct his decisions. Your values must show up in your calendar and your checkbook for them to be real values; otherwise they are just wishes or ideals. Your values help you distinguish between truly important things (for you) and something that is urgently vying for your attention (but not a of high value). **Have**

you identified your values? If so, are you talking about them or are they making their way into your daily schedule? *Lord, You have done a work in me to establish values that are important to me. Now I want to make room for the expression of those values in my daily life. Help me to distinguish between the important and urgent, and then give me the courage and strength to make the important things my highest priorities.*

March 10
More Values

"If others have this right of support from you, shouldn't we have it all the more? But we did not use this right. On the contrary, we put up with anything rather than hinder the gospel of Christ"
- 1 Corinthians 9:12.

Paul worked while he ministered and the decision to do so came from his value of not taking support from the churches he planted. The other apostles took this support to which they were entitled, but Paul did not, raising the money for his entire team. Somehow, somewhere, Paul developed a governing value to work to support his ministry. That is an excellent example of how governing values guide your daily decisions. **Do you have values that can direct your daily decisions to this extent? What are they? Have you described and prioritized them? Perhaps you should write them down?** *Lord, it is so much easier putting my decisions on You, saying "The Lord told me to do this or that." Yet I am seeing here that Paul's heart told him what to do based on what You had worked into his life. I want that same dynamic in my life. Please help me see and act on what is important to me based on Your work in my heart.*

March 11
Elegant and Simple

"But now that there is no more place for me to work in these regions, and since I have been longing for many years to visit you, I plan to do so when I go to Spain. I hope to see you while passing through and to have you assist me on my journey there, after I have enjoyed your company for a while" - Romans 15:23-25.

Paul had a value not to work in another man's field but only to go where no church existed. That value determined for him that his work was finished in the areas where he had been, and it was therefore time to go to Spain. He would stop in Rome on the way, not to plant a church but to simply visit the saints. What an elegant and simple plan, and that is an example of what values will and can do for you, your lifestyle and your time management. **Do you have elegant and simple values that can direct your decisions and time use as Paul did? Do you see values as spiritual and capable of simplifying your life's work? Can you trust your values to guide your daily decisions?** *Lord, I want to be led by Your Spirit and I now see that You can identify and establish a value in my life and that value can then do Your work of leading and guiding me on a daily basis. I can trust this process because You are not trying to trick me, but want me to know and do Your will. Thank You for Your work in me.*

March 12
Interrupted

"The Gibeonites then sent word to Joshua in the camp at Gilgal: 'Do not abandon your servants.

Come up to us quickly and save us! Help us, because all the Amorite kings from the hill country have joined forces against us.' So Joshua marched up from Gilgal with his entire army, including all the best fighting men" - Joshua 10:6-7.

Joshua's routine was interrupted with this urgent message from his allies. Interruptions and emergencies are a part of life. You can try to arrange not to be disturbed, but sometimes they are inevitable. Over the next few days you will look at this story in Joshua and see how he handled his time and what his thinking was in the process. **How do you handle interruptions? Are they the rule for your day? Do you get uptight when you are interrupted? Do you have trouble focusing after the interruption?** *Lord, I realize interruptions are a way of life, but I need help handling them more effectively than I am right now. I either get upset over the interruption or I surrender to it, thus throwing my day off kilter and rendering some days virtually useless, which again upsets me. Help me with this common but annoying problem!*

March 13
One Hour Less

"The Lord said to Joshua, 'Do not be afraid of them; I have given them into your hand. Not one of them will be able to withstand you.' After an all-night march from Gilgal, Joshua took them by surprise" - Joshua 10:8-9.

The Lord promised Joshua a great victory and the Lord certainly did His part to bring that about. Yet Joshua and his men had to do their part and their part was to miss a night's sleep (or two). God spoke, they marched and then they fought. **While proper rest is critical for you, how much is 'proper'? Have you convinced yourself you need more sleep than you really do? What could you do with one hour less sleep a day, which could translate into an hour to write, study or learn?** One hour a day adds up to seven hours every week, or 354 hours a year, which is almost fifteen 24-hour days! *Lord, sometimes I must lose sleep to pursue something You have put before me to do. I trust You for the energy and alertness I need to do the job! Help me not to talk myself into fatigue or laziness, and give me the same spirit Joshua had as he took his enemies by surprise after an all-night march.*

March 14
The Difference

"The Lord threw them into confusion before Israel, so Joshua and the Israelites defeated them completely at Gibeon. Israel pursued them along the road going up to Beth Horon and cut them down all the way to Azekah and Makkedah. As they fled before Israel on the road down from Beth Horon to Azekah, the Lord hurled large hailstones down on them, and more of them died from the hail than were killed by the swords of the Israelites"
- Joshua 10:10-11.

Joshua did what he could do - marched all night - and that freed the Lord to do what only He could do - bring about a great victory. Many are waiting for God to do what only they can do or trying to do for themselves what only God can do. People who successfully manage their time know the difference and act accordingly. **Do you sense God's help in your daily activities? Are you worn out or fired up? Do you know the difference**

between your role and God's and are you acting on them in faith? *Lord, I need You to throw some hailstones on my enemies. The ones like fear, laziness and presumption. I also need You to help me understand my role in our partnership on a daily basis. Help me to know what I should be doing so that I can then behold the help that only You can provide, just like Joshua did in this story.*

March 15
Stopping the Sun

"On the day the Lord gave the Amorites over to Israel, Joshua said to the Lord in the presence of Israel: 'Sun, stand still over Gibeon, and you, moon, over the Valley of Aijalon.' So the sun stood still, and the moon stopped, till the nation avenged itself on its enemies" **- Joshua 10:12-13**

When Joshua saw the great opportunity he had but time moving on, he prayed for more time. He did not pray that God would help him, but prayed that the sun would stand still so he could finish the task. What great faith he had to believe that time would stop for his cause and work. Yet that was the work God had given Him, so He was asking God to do His part as Joshua did his. **What do you pray about where time is concerned? Do you have faith for time? Do you give up on projects because you don't have time (or think you don't)? Or do you trust God to help you get it done?** *Lord, You are a miracle-working God, and I have learned today that I can trust you for time and trust You to make even more time. Yet in this case You did not make more time, You caused light to be prolonged so Joshua could work all night. I ask that You do the same for me as I labor to finish Your projects.*

March 16
Impossible

"The sun stopped in the middle of the sky and delayed going down about a full day. There has never been a day like it before or since, a day when the Lord listened to a human being. Surely the Lord was fighting for Israel!" - Joshua 10:13b-14.

Joshua marched all night to engage the enemy and, when he did, there was so much to do that he prayed and the sun stood still for an entire day. That means he and the army went without sleep for two whole nights. What's more, they were physically involved in battle for 72 hours. They were probably exhausted, but did the seemingly impossible with God's help. **What can you do with just a little less sleep? What are you considering physically impossible that is possible with the right mindset and faith in God's help? What more can you do than you are doing now?** *Lord, I put many things in the 'impossible' category that are possible with Your help. When I consider them 'impossible,' I don't even attempt them, putting limits on what I can do for You. Open my eyes to see where I have attached the label 'impossible' so I can remove that label and act, trusting You to make it 'possible.'*

March 17
Dis-Couraged

"Joshua said to them, 'Do not be afraid; do not be discouraged. Be strong and courageous. This is what the Lord will do to all the enemies you are going to fight'" - Joshua 10:20.

Even though Joshua and his army had fought for 72

hours with great results, they were still discouraged at what had to be done. Discouragement will sap your energy and cause you to look for ways to shut down before the book is written, the language is learned or the business is prospering. When you are dis-couraged, the only antidote is to be en-couraged, and that means to summon courage to act when everything in you does not want to do so. **Are you discouraged? What can you do to get back on track? If you talked yourself into dis-couragement, how can you talk yourself into en-couragement?** *Lord, I am grateful for what I have been able to do, but there is so much more and I am discouraged, which means I have lost heart. I choose to get back on track and be encouraged, with Your help. I choose to focus on what You have done instead of what I have yet to do, trusting You to finish the task.*

March 18
Grace

"But by the grace of God I am what I am, and his grace to me was not without effect. No, I worked harder than all of them—yet not I, but the grace of God that was with me"
- 1 Corinthians 15:10.

Paul knew what to do with his time and you have to admit that he made quite an impact on the world using the time he had available. He did this not only by working hard, but also working hard at the right things. Often hard work means long hours of work and Paul discovered a secret, which was to allow God's grace to work through and with him. **Do you sense God's grace working with you as you labor? Do long hours take away more than they give back? Are those hours filled with meaningful work or meaningless trivia?**

Lord, I want to know and feel that partnership between my work and Your grace. I am not afraid of hard work, but I want my hours to count. May Your presence energize me and give me courage to do Your work!

March 19
A Little Less

"I have labored and toiled and have often gone without sleep; I have known hunger and thirst and have often gone without food; I have been cold and naked. Besides everything else, I face daily the pressure of my concern for all the churches"
- 2 Corinthians 11:27-28.

If you put Paul into a special category of a 'super man,' you will miss the lesson for your life. Paul did more than he thought possible and you can too! He worked under extreme pressure, yet was able to be productive and accomplish much. **If Paul can do all that, what more can you do than you are doing now? What small changes in your time management, like a little less sleep, a little less television, a little less time doing nothing, can reap large returns in doing what is in your heart to do?** *Lord, I look at Paul's life and I marvel at what he did. Yet he was human just like me, who also happened to be filled with Your Spirit. If Paul could do all that, I need to find out what I can do. I know it is more than I am doing now. Help me make the changes I need to make to be as effective in my day as Paul was in his.*

March 20
Stop To Do

"Then he went upstairs again and broke bread and ate. After talking until daylight, he left" - Acts 20:11.

Paul knew how to establish priorities and follow them, even when it meant losing some sleep. You also may not have to lose sleep, but in order to do some things you have never done, you will have to stop doing things you are now doing. In other words, you may need a stop-to-do list before you create a to-do list. **What is it that you have been wanting to do? What is it that you have wanted to stop doing? How can you stop the one so you can engage the other? What is stopping you from doing both?** *Lord, I know I have 24 hours every day and, while my possibilities are endless, my time is not. Therefore I must make some tough decisions of what to do and what to **stop** doing. Yet I am attached to some of those things I currently do, so I need Your help to break away from the familiar into the unknown.*

March 21
To Do List

"The Lord said to him, 'Go back the way you came, and go to the Desert of Damascus. When you get there, anoint Hazael king over Aram. Also, anoint Jehu son of Nimshi king over Israel, and anoint Elisha son of Shaphat from Abel Meholah to succeed you as prophet'" - 1 Kings 19:15-16.

In a sense, the Lord created a to-do list for Elijah, giving him things He needed to do along with the order in which they needed to be done. You also need this kind of list to help you focus, otherwise it is like someone throwing more than one ball to you at a time. You don't know which one to catch, so they all fall to ground. **Are you in the habit of making a list of what you need and would like to do? Do you then establish priorities on the list, determining which thing you would do first, second, etc.?** *Lord, there are times when I lose my daily* focus, and consequently waste time by doing nothing because there is so much I could be doing. I need Your help first to discipline myself so I can create a list, then help to focus on my priorities. Finally, I need Your assistance to follow through on those prioritized tasks.

March 22
Focus

"So Elisha left him and went back. He took his yoke of oxen and slaughtered them. He burned the plowing equipment to cook the meat and gave it to the people, and they ate. Then he set out to follow Elijah and became his servant" - 1 Kings 19:21.

Elijah went from the cave to do one thing on this to-do list and that was to anoint his successor. When he found him, Elisha was busy plowing a field with some oxen. He accepted the call, slaughtered the oxen and burned the yokes. He eliminated all distractions so he could focus on the task at hand and become Elijah's servant. **Do you have that kind of focus? Maybe it is because you permit too many distractions to be around you, which vie for your attention?** *Lord, sometimes I allow the distractions in my life because I **want** to lose focus. I am afraid to do what is before me, so I listen to the other 'voices' that call my name. I need the determination and focus Elisha had. Help me to deal with the things in me that give the distractions entrance and attention.*

March 23
Delegation

"You have made them to be a kingdom and priests to serve our God, and they will reign on the earth" - Revelation 5:10.

Your destiny is to rule on the earth, not just in the next age, but also in this one. To be effective, kings focus on what is most important and don't waste time on trivialities. In other words, kings must rule their time and that means they focus on what is most important, delegating everything else to others. Yet giving things to others to do can be a challenge, because you think no one can do them as well as you. You also may want to maintain control of your life, and the only way you know to do that is to do things yourself. **How effectively do you delegate to others? Do you see delegation as dangerous and painful, or as something necessary for you to rule your time and sphere of influence?** *Lord, I don't share duties with others very well, preferring to do things myself for many reasons, some of them legitimate, some of them selfish. Also, my need to control my world is fear-based and I need to release some of what I do so I can do other more important things. Help me to let go and let others do their work!*

March 24
Bottleneck

"When his father-in-law saw all that Moses was doing for the people, he said, 'What is this you are doing for the people? Why do you alone sit as judge, while all these people stand around you from morning till evening?'" - Exodus 18:14.

Moses was a busy man, but he was alone in his work. He had no vision or concept of the importance of and strategy for involving others. In other words, he tried to do the work of 100 people rather than find 100 people to do it. This was not only hard on Moses, but also on those who were affected by the bottleneck he had created. **Are you working long hours, wearing yourself out** because of your sense that you have to do the work yourself? Do you feel guilt when you aren't doing the work? When you don't show up, do you also feel guilty or like you are somehow being 'left out'? *Lord, I am emotionally attached to my position and my work. Consequently, I can't let go! I know it is taking a toll on me and others, but I am afraid to let go. First, help me to get my thinking straight that I am not the only one who can do good work. Then show me the people to whom I can give my work.*

March 25
Fatigue

"Moses' father-in-law replied, 'What you are doing is not good. You and these people who come to you will only wear yourselves out. The work is too heavy for you; you cannot handle it alone'"
- Exodus 18:17-18.

You don't have to be busy to be exhausted. Fatigue can be caused by mental weariness. When you don't delegate, it wears everyone out - those with whom you work, those whom you serve and you. Jethro made the evaluation that this situation was 'not good' in this passage. **Are you exhausted? Is lack of delegating the possible cause? Is it time you change your work habits and philosophy, which would mean changing the way you use your time?** *Lord, I am tired and it's not a good tired. I am fatigued because of mental strain from trying to do too much, from being a perfectionist and not learning how to let go and let others. This is 'not good' and I want to change. Show me how and I vow to follow through and regain my energy level that I need and want.*

March 26
Time for God

"Listen now to me and I will give you some advice, and may God be with you. You must be the people's representative before God and bring their disputes to him" - Exodus 18:19.

Moses' father-in-law gave him some good advice to stop doing all the work and establish clear priorities based on what it was that only he (Moses) could do, allowing others to do what they could do. Moses needed to spend more time with the Lord and less time with the people. That is good advice for you and me too. **How is your prayer life? Do you spend the time you want and need in God's Word? Are you taking time to think about what you are doing and need to do?** *Lord, I am busy with all kinds of things that take me away from You, my Source of wisdom, strength, encouragement, and discernment. I need to do what Moses did, and that is to spend a little more time with You sorting out my world, getting what I require from You for the work You have assigned me to do.*

March 27
Your Team

"Teach them his decrees and instructions, and show them the way they are to live and how they are to behave" - Exodus 18:20.

Jethro continued to help Moses focus his work priorities as opposed to doing it all himself. As we saw yesterday, first, he urged Moses to spend more time in prayer, representing the people before God. Then Jethro directed him to pick his team to whom he would delegate, spending some time to train them in the work. **Are you still trying to do the work of many people instead of finding many people to do the work? Who is, or should be, part of your team? How can you apply these principles of delegation and team building to your family, work or ministry?** *Lord, I am reluctant to release my work to others, for fear they won't do as good of a job as I. Then there is the fear of picking the right people. Show me my 'world' as You see it, and then help me identify the right people. Finally, help me prepare them, even my children, for the work at hand.*

March 28
Your Load

"Have them serve as judges for the people at all times, but have them bring every difficult case to you; the simple cases they can decide themselves. That will make your load lighter, because they will share it with you" - Exodus 18:21.

When you delegate, it is not to dump undesirable tasks onto someone else. It is so that you can focus on doing what it is that you do best and are most gifted to do. Plus, you have a 'load' of duties to carry but others are to help you carry that load to make it lighter. **Are you under a heavy load? Do you have grace to carry your load or is it weighing you down spiritually and emotionally? What changes do you need to make to lighten your load?** *Lord, my load of work and responsibility is too much for me and that means I am doing something wrong. I have taken on too much and need to find others to help me with the tasks, or explain to my supervisors or family that the work is too much. Give me the insight and courage I need to be able to lighten my load.*

March 29
Inner Peace

"If you do this and God so commands, you will be able to stand the strain, and all these people will go home satisfied" - Exodus 18:23.

The benefits of God-directed delegation are many, but the main ones are inner peace and satisfaction in and from the work God has assigned you to do. As we conclude our discussion of delegation, examine once again what is keeping you from delegating. **Is it perfectionism? Is it fear? Is it ignorance? Is it not having enough good people in your world to whom you can give the tasks?** If you address those issues today, then next year at this time you won't be so overwhelmed and your work will take on new meaning and significance. *Lord, I know I need to let go and let others do what they can do. I have held on to my duties too tightly, drawing my identity from them and even becoming emotionally attached to them. It's time for some changes to the way I work, and I ask Your help as I make significant adjustments to my work and lifestyle.*

March 30
Sleepwalking

"He who gathers crops in summer is a prudent son, but he who sleeps during harvest is a disgraceful son" - Proverbs 10:5.

As we near the end of this month's theme of time management, we return once again to the issue of priorities and your ability to recognize and follow through on those things that are most important to you and the work God has assigned you. When it's harvest time, everything else has to be put on hold so the harvest can be gathered and not lost. **Do you have that kind of urgency around important tasks? Or do you find excuses not to do them, as if sleepwalking through your day? What is keeping you from those highest priority activities?** *Lord, I feel like I am sleepwalking through my days, putting off until tomorrow what needs to be done today. There is a harvest of opportunities before me and I am missing the harvest somehow. Help me respond with urgency to the matters before me so that I won't miss my harvest of fruitful work.*

March 31
Urgency

"How long will you lie there, you sluggard? When will you get up from your sleep? A little sleep, a little slumber, a little folding of the hands to rest— and poverty will come on you like a thief and scarcity like an armed man" - Proverbs 6:9-11.

This month you have studied principles to help you manage your time, or manage the events that fill the time you have. Now it's up to you to apply those principles so that you can do the things that are in your heart to do. No one can make you do this; you must do it for yourself. Otherwise time will pass you by and your best intentions will remain unfulfilled and untouched. **What are your main 'takeaways' from this month's discussion? What changes will you make? What are your main objectives you want to achieve with your improved time management skills? Where will you place the urgency in your life and work?** *Lord, I thank You for Your help this month as I have addressed my need for time management training. Now help me* *apply the principles as I seek to improve. I want to be productive and fulfilled, and I know that comes from You and from my diligence in pursuing Your will. I commit my way to You and ask Your help.*

April

Gold Mine Principle 4

Organization

April 1
Organized

*"Locusts have no king,
yet they advance together in ranks"
- Proverbs 30:27.*

God has put the ability to organize in **all** His creation, including the insect kingdom, as today's verse indicates. That also includes you and me. How you organize will determine how well you can stay on top of the duties and responsibilities God has given you. That organization must include your paperwork, computer files, transportation, living quarters, relationships and daily activities. **Are you pleased with your personal organization? What areas need attention? What bias, if any, do you have against organization that may be keeping you from being like the locust, which has the ability to structure its world?** *Lord, I need to be better organized, for too often I am looking for things I need but can't find them. As it is now, I cannot handle any more of whatever it is You want to give me, and that is not good. Help me this month to develop new habits and disciplines that will enable my life to have better structure and order.*

April 2
The Desire

*"Go to the ant, you sluggard;
consider its ways and be wise!
It has no commander, no overseer or ruler,
yet it stores its provisions in summer
and gathers its food at harvest" - Proverbs 6:6-8.*

You learned yesterday that the ability to organize is

in all God's' creation, including you. What's missing sometimes is the desire. You must learn to organize your world, not just to be a 'neat-nik,' but to remove clutter that leads to stress and inability to fulfill your purpose and goals. Last month you looked at time management. This month you will look at principles to help structure your world for greater effectiveness and peace of mind. **Are you willing to learn to organize? Are you ready to draw on the innate ability you have to bring structure to your life and things? Is this something you want or feel pressured to do?** *Lord, I confess that I have enjoyed some of my disorganization, which in a sense is being rebellious on my part. My life and the things in it have not reflected Your will, and my disorganization has kept me attached to my stuff and unable to embrace new opportunities You have for me. I am ready and willing to change.*

April 3
Like God

"For God is not a God of disorder but of peace— as in all the congregations of the Lord's people" - 1 Corinthians 14:33.

God is a God of order. We know what day summer will begin and end. We know what time the sun will come up and go down every day. We can tell what time high and low tides will occur. Yet all this order does not diminish or take away from God's great creativity. **So, if God is a God of order and you are not an orderly person, then is your disorder an ungodly trait? If you have learned to be unorganized, can you learn new skills that will release your latent organizing skills and thus enhance your creativity? Do you need to repent of your disorganization and ask God's help?** *Lord, I* have rejoiced in my ability to create, but I have at times feared being organized would somehow make me less creative! Yet You are both organized **and** creative and I see I need to be just like You. Forgive me for treating my 'world' like it was exclusively mine and not making room for Your order.

April 4
The Spirit's Help

"For the Spirit God gave us does not make us timid, but gives us power, love and self-discipline"
- 2 Timothy 1:7.

So far you have learned that God has given all His creation the ability to organize and that God Himself loves order. The only thing stopping you from being organized is either lack of training or desire. In this verse today you see that God is ready and willing to help you through the Spirit by giving you power, love and the discipline to do His will, including organizing your duties and things. You are not alone when you organize! **Have you asked the Spirit for the power to organize your life? Can you see how your organization can be an expression of love to those around you? Do you want the self-discipline the Spirit can give for your organizational skills?** *Lord, I lack the discipline to be organized, but I know You can assist me. I ask You today for that help! Help me structure my world in love and power so I can serve You and others beyond what is possible in my own strength!*

April 5
Traveling Light

"When you come, bring the cloak that I left with

> ***Carpus at Troas, and my scrolls, especially the parchments" - 2 Timothy 4:13.***

Paul traveled light and had to do so because of the nature of his work. You should have the same philosophy. Your life is probably cluttered with things that you no longer use, things that you are keeping *just in case* you need them or things to which you are emotionally attached. A good rule to follow is this: When in doubt, throw it out. **Do you have too much stuff? Is it time to go room by room, closet by closet, and have a garage sale or give things away?** What is keeping you from doing that? Perhaps this is where you need to start in your quest to be more organized. *Lord, I confess I have a hard time getting rid of my stuff, including papers, clothes, tools and more. I need to lighten my load to travel light in the work You gave me to do, so I commit to getting rid of what is weighing me down. Help me to get over my attachment to things.*

April 6
Organization Defined

> ***"We took such a violent battering from the storm that the next day they began to throw the cargo overboard" - Acts 27:18.***

When the going got tough, the sailors on the ship taking Paul to Rome had to jettison cargo to make it through the storm. That is the same principle you must follow. The definition for organization is: "The removal of all clutter, whether physical or mental, in order that you may give your attention to your highest priority activity at any given point in time." **How cluttered is your physical space - car, desk, home, computer, closets? Is your clutter making you go through work to get to** work? Do you spend time looking for things? is your mind free to think and create or is it preoccupied?** *Lord, my world is cluttered, not only outside of me, but inside as well. I am carrying too much baggage and it is keeping me from doing what You have for me to do. I need to streamline my world and it starts today. With Your help, I will remove my clutter this month.*

April 7
Act Like Royalty

"A large population is a king's glory, but without subjects a prince is ruined" - Proverbs 14:28.

You are a son or daughter of the King, making you a prince or princess. God has equipped you to want and handle more so that you will extend God's kingdom through your work, life and ministry. If you are disorganized, however, you will not be able to handle what you have let alone more. **Do you have a philosophy and system to organize what you have - time, belongings, work, relationships? Do you want one or are you happy with a haphazard approach to today and tomorrow?** *Lord, in some sense I am royalty, but I am not acting like it. My life is not a reflection at this point of Your call and I need to make some changes. Give me a strategy to organize my 'world' so that I may handle the royal calling that is mine. Give me the desire and ability to rule over more than I have now.*

April 8
Peace

"For God is not a God of disorder but of peace— as in all the congregations of the Lord's people" - 1 Corinthians 14:33.

We looked at this verse a few days ago, but there is one more thing to see before we move on. Notice that in this verse the opposite of disorder is not order but peace. So the things you have and do should bring peace to you and others. If you are on time for appointments and you can find what you need to do your work quickly, then your organizational system is working and should produce peace. **When you behold your schedule, your closets, your workspace, and your work, does it bring a sense of fulfillment and peace? Or do you feel guilty and scattered? Are you wasting long amounts of time looking for things, putting off what needs to be done because you can't find what you need to do them?** *Lord, I want and need peace in my life, a peace that carries over to others as they work with me. That means I can't keep people waiting or break my promises because I can't organize my time, my family, my files or my possessions. Give me wisdom to be able to produce peace from the disorder that has been a habit in my life.*

April 9
Possibilities

"Now the earth was formless and empty, darkness was over the surface of the deep, and the Spirit of God was hovering over the waters"
- Genesis 1:2.

The Hebrew concept in this verse is that the earth had great potential and the Spirit came to bring it to its fullness. Thus the chaos was not the enemy of order here, but rather partnered with the order to bring about what we have today. The Spirit is present to create order out of your chaos, too, but you must let go of the chaos if you want to release your potential. **What is** keeping you from structuring your world to be more productive? What are you afraid of? Do you really believe you have great possibilities in the midst of your confusion and chaos? *Lord, I invite Your Spirit into my chaos, for You see the possibilities that I cannot see. I do surrender, however, to the work that needs to be done, and I realize that this is for my own good! I will never fulfill Your plans for me unless I allow You access and order this chaos. So, I choose to let go of my chaos today and can't wait to see the results.*

April 10
Your Stuff

"John answered, 'Anyone who has two shirts should share with the one who has none, and anyone who has food should do the same'" - Luke 3:11.

When you start to organize your world, you may realize that you have too much stuff, and that your stuff owns you instead of you owning it. There is an adage to follow when considering whether or not you should keep something: "When in doubt, throw it out!" Of course, 'throwing it out' may mean giving it away to someone else or having a yard sale to give the proceeds to the poor or missions. **Do you have too much stuff? Is the thought of parting with some of your belongings difficult to think about? Does your stuff own you - you are attached to it and cannot part with it even though you don't use or need it?** *Lord, I am attached to some of my possessions in an unhealthy manner. I keep moving things around to try and make more room, and the clutter is distracting to others and me. I need to streamline my world so I can be more focused, but it's difficult. I need Your help for my things control me instead of Your Spirit.*

April 11
Purposeful Organization

"When the queen of Sheba heard about the fame of Solomon and his relationship to the Lord, she came to test Solomon with hard questions" - 1 Kings 10:1.

The queen came from Ethiopia to see and hear Solomon. God may want to give you a reputation in your field that is a blessing to others as you share your wealth of knowledge and experience. Yet disorganization and clutter can prevent you from developing your purpose into what it can be, and keep you from maximizing your purpose for the Lord once you develop it. **Are you thinking in terms of organizing your world to develop your potential? Are you organizing your world so that you can maximize your impact and influence for the Lord on others?** *Lord, You have given me a purpose and I am to maximize the influence and skill that comes with it. Yet I know clutter and disorganization can keep me from doing all that You want me to do. It's time I stopped playing small, and rose up to the full stature of what You have for me. Help me to order my world accordingly.*

April 12
Large

"Arriving at Jerusalem with a very great caravan—with camels carrying spices, large quantities of gold, and precious stones—she came to Solomon and talked with him about all that she had on her mind" - 1 Kings 10:2.

The queen traveled with a large entourage, and Solomon received her into his world that was also substantial. The point here is that both had organized to be able to handle all over which they had oversight and responsibility. You are also created to handle more, but lack of organization can thwart your growth. **Do you see that God may want to give you more than you have now? Do you want more? Are you prepared to stretch and grow to learn how to handle and oversee it, whether the more is duties, responsibility, staff, family or money?** *Lord, I don't know how I feel about growing 'large.' I am comfortable with my world being manageable and small, but that may not be Your will. I need to pay attention to what You want me to do and how I need to organize my life, time and belongings to help make that happen.*

April 13
Opportunities

"Solomon answered all her questions; nothing was too hard for the king to explain to her"
- 1 Kings 10:3.

Solomon received the queen and spent a great deal of time with her. To be able to do that, Solomon had to organize his world to free up his time, and to prepare in advance. Tomorrow you will see how the queen reacted to all this, but in the meantime, you can see here that organization allowed Solomon to take advantage of a great opportunity to impact a world leader when she came calling. **Are you organized to take advantage of opportunities that come your way? Does the peace that results from your lack of clutter help you focus and prepare yourself for future opportunities?** *Lord, You know the future; I don't. Therefore You can help me today to prepare for the opportunities of tomorrow. Help me to organize in faith, and then to recognize those* opportunities when they come along. Also, help me to prepare myself today so I can maximize my impact for You tomorrow.

April 14
Big

"When the queen of Sheba saw all the wisdom of Solomon and the palace he had built, the food on his table, the seating of his officials, the attending servants in their robes, his cupbearers, and the burnt offerings he made at the temple of the Lord, she was overwhelmed" - 1 Kings 10:4-5.

The queen traveled with a big entourage, so she was accustomed to protocol, pomp and ceremony, along with the detailed planning that went with them all. Yet what she saw at Solomon's court overwhelmed her. The size and order of it all made a profound impression on her. **When is the last time that someone was overwhelmed by your work, your church or your household, especially the scope and order of it? Would you like to be a part of something that regal and organized? Do you see that Solomon's God-given wisdom helped to shape and fashion what the queen saw?** *Lord, 'big' may intimidate me but it doesn't do that to You. My ability to organize more effectively is learning how to draw on Your wisdom of how to structure and order my 'world.' I want to be part of a work that overwhelms others in a good way for Your purpose and glory. Help me to think and produce 'big.'*

April 15
Reputation

"She said to the king, 'The report I heard in my own

country about your achievements and your wisdom is true. But I did not believe these things until I came and saw with my own eyes. Indeed, not even half was told me; in wisdom and wealth you have far exceeded the report I heard'" - 1 Kings 10:6-7.

It is of note that Solomon's organizational prowess had gained a reputation that was discussed the world over in his day. Such is the impact of an organization that is committed to excellence not as an end unto itself, but as a means to release the purpose of the individual or the organization. This leads us back to your organizational philosophy, which should be about more than just keeping things in place. **What is your reputation where organization is concerned? Do you organize so that you can be effective for the Lord's work? Does your ability to get things done attract the attention of others?** *Lord, I want to be known for my purpose and I further want my organization to add to, and not take away from, my ability to serve You. Help me develop an organizational philosophy that will cover my time, things and priorities. I want others to have confidence in my ability to organize to be a valued team member.*

April 16
Worship

"Praise be to the Lord your God, who has delighted in you and placed you on the throne of Israel. Because of the Lord's eternal love for Israel, he has made you king to maintain justice and righteousness" - 1 Kings 10:9.

The Queen was not part of Israel, but when she beheld Solomon's wisdom against a backdrop of his kingdom's organization, she praised God for what she saw. **When** has an unbeliever broken into worship because of what they saw in your world and life? Do you see that Solomon's organization was not the end in itself, but a means for him to fulfill his purpose and maintain justice in his kingdom? What purpose does your organization support and promote? *Lord, Solomon was effective in part because he organized his world to handle and be able to do more. I want to follow his example and structure all I have in such a way that You will be honored and glorified by my resulting productivity, so that others may see and worship You. Give me wisdom and grace to do that.*

April 17
More

"(Hiram's ships brought gold from Ophir; and from there they brought great cargoes of almugwood and precious stones. The king used the almugwood to make supports for the temple of the Lord and for the royal palace, and to make harps and lyres for the musicians. So much almugwood has never been imported or seen since that day)" - 1 Kings 10:11-12.

Let's review. You have learned so far that you should not have to go through work to get to work. That means you may have too much stuff, so when in doubt, throw it out to stay streamlined and nimble. Yet God may want to give you more responsibility as you see in today's passage, so you must have an organizational strategy or philosophy that enables you to handle more than you have now. That means that 'more' is not always wrong, but may be God's will. **Are you growing in your understanding of why organization is important? What changes have you made, or do you need to make, to be better organized for God's purpose?**

Lord, I am learning much about Your desire for me to organize my world so I can be effective with the opportunities I have and be prepared for new ones to come. Yet I have a long way to go, and I need Your help to want 'more' and then to change so I can handle 'more,' whatever that 'more' may be.

April 18
Oxen

"Where there are no oxen, the manger is empty, but from the strength of an ox come abundant harvests" - Proverbs 14:4.

You may have an empty manger, so you don't have much to organize and oversee. That doesn't indicate you are organized; it just means you have reduced or kept your world to its most manageable components. If that's the case, then you must ask: **What will it take for you to be more productive? How can you obtain oxen to produce a harvest, a harvest that may involve helping others, creating art, writing or starting your own business, whether small or big?** *Lord, I have kept my world simple for fear that I will not be able to manage any more. In some sense, I am afraid of success not failure. I don't have any 'oxen' because I don't want to be bothered with learning how to care for more so I can do more. Help me to expand my thinking so I can expand my world.*

April 19
Vision

"Where there is no [vision], people cast off restraint; but blessed is the one who heeds wisdom's instruction" - Proverbs 29:18.

You need wisdom and divine insight to help you organize today for tomorrow's opportunities. What's more, you need a vision for your life and purpose to organize for maximum effectiveness. For instance, **if you are a painter, where will your studio or work area be? If you are a writer, where will you write and what can you do with that space to make it creativity-friendly? If you are a counselor, how can you organize your day, notes and contact with clients and peers?** *Lord, I need a vision for my life so I can plan today for where I will be tomorrow. I ask You for wisdom to put things in place not just so they won't get lost, but so I can find them when I need them, and so they can all flow together with my purpose and daily work.*

April 20
Resisting Change

"He is working in you. God is helping you obey Him. God is doing what He wants done in you"
- Philippians 2:13 (WEB).

You may be reading these for organizational tips, but one thing is certain: If you are to be more organized, you must change from the inside out. And you can resist the change because it takes you out of your comfort zone where things are uncertain and failure is possible. Yet when you resist change, you are trying to control your life and world in an unhealthy way, stunting your growth and development. **Are you resisting internal change where organization is concerned? What is it costing you in lost opportunities? What are you willing to do about it?** *Lord, I recognize I have been blocking my own development by resisting change, and I have found excuses and actually made them sound spiritual! In a sense I am placing the blame for my lack of change* on You! Forgive me, Lord, for You are working in me to change and I commit to cooperate with Your work.

April 21
Faithful

***"However that which is spiritual isn't first, but that which is natural, then that which is spiritual"
- 1 Corinthians 15:46.***

You may be thinking, "I'm not sure how relevant my organizational habits are to my spiritual life." According to today's verse, they are highly relevant, for you prepare for and prove your spiritual maturity by mastering natural things. After all, if God speaks something to you and you are so disorganized that you forget or fail to follow through because of confusion, you render yourself spiritually ineffective. **Do you see that the natural and spiritual are connected? Can you see how your disorganization has spiritual implications?** *Lord, there are no shortcuts to effectiveness in You. I must first prove myself in the natural and then You will bestow spiritual responsibilities on me. Part of faithfulness is my ability to organize my life, money, time and possessions. Give me wisdom, insight and vision to do that.*

April 22
Proverbs

". . . when he gave the sea its boundary so the waters would not overstep his command, and when he marked out the foundations of the earth. Then I [wisdom] was constantly at his side. I was filled with delight day after day, rejoicing always in his presence, rejoicing in his whole world and delighting in mankind" - Proverbs 8:29-31.

God used divine wisdom to structure and organize the world as you can see from today's passage. This wisdom is personal and loves God's creation. Thus you can draw on wisdom to help you organize your world. **Where do you get this wisdom?** One place is the book of Proverbs. Therefore you should study the book of Proverbs regularly to find nuggets of organizational wisdom for your life. **Did you realize that if you read a chapter from Proverbs every day, you will finish the book once a month and twelve times a year? Why not start reading a chapter today with the intent of searching for tips on how to plan and structure your life?** *Lord, all Your word is important and Proverbs is especially important for my daily life. Give me the discipline to read it every day and then give me the insight to sort through its many topics to see material that will help me organize my world, just as wisdom helped You organize Your world.*

April 23
Time and Events

"Then he [Paul] went upstairs again and broke bread and ate. After talking until daylight, he left"
- Acts 20:11.

Paul organized his time to maximize his impact on churches he planted and visited. In March you studied time management and found out it is a misnomer; you don't manage time, but rather the events that fill it. Obviously organization and time management go hand in hand, so perhaps a review of last month's Pearls will contribute toward your organizational emphasis this month. **Are you happy with your time or event management? Are you doing the most important things or just staying busy? What changes do you** need to make to use your time more effectively? *Lord, I have 24 hours every day, and I must pay attention to how I am using them as part of my organizational philosophy. Give me new skills and awareness where time is concerned so I can structure my day to achieve my highest priority events according to Your will for me.*

April 24
A Clean Manger

"Where there are no oxen, the manger is empty, but from the strength of an ox come abundant harvests" - Proverbs 14:4.

Your life may be simpler without technology, but it isn't easier to organize without it. While technology brings its own set of problems, just like a messy ox, it also enables you to do so much more and organize all that you do. Plus, technology can do some of the organizing for you, just like an ox does things for the farmer he cannot do for himself. Keep in mind: You don't have to understand how the technology works, you only have to know how to use it. **What is your level of skill with technology? Are you intimidated by it? If you are comfortable with it, are you learning new things to better organize your day and work?** *Lord, You created technology. I admit that I am fearful of it and have tried to keep a clean manger, so to speak, to avoid any mess. I am willing, however, to learn and grow. Help me find people who will tutor me, then help me identify what I need for the work I am doing, and finally, help me use it effectively.*

April 25
Lighten the Load

"So they got up and fled in the dusk and abandoned

their tents and their horses and donkeys. They left the camp as it was and ran for their lives"
- 2 Kings 7:7.

The enemies of Israel thought they were in danger, so they fled, leaving behind all their stuff because it weighed them down. **Is your stuff weighing you down?** Earlier in the month, we used a phrase to help guide how you treat your stuff: When in doubt, throw it out. One study showed that 87% of what you save (articles, paper, reports, files, old clothes, etc.) is never used or referred to again! **Has it been a while since you cleaned up your world by discarding what you have not worn, looked at or used in a long time? How soon can you set aside some time to streamline the world of your computer, desk, office, attic, work space or purse?** *Lord, I know I have too much stuff and it is weighing me down, not allowing me to be nimble and free. I commit to go through my world room by room, desk by desk, closet by closet and computer by computer to lighten my load as I go forward and progress in Your will for my life.*

April 26
Hired Help

"The reason I left you in Crete was that you might put in order what was left unfinished and appoint elders in every town, as I directed you" - Titus 1:5.

Sometimes you need other people to help you organize. Perhaps you need to hire a housekeeper, driver, gardener, or personal assistant to do some things for you to relieve some of the pressure on your time and your gifting, which may not include organization. **What is stopping you from expanding the people in your** world who work for you? Is it only money? Or is there a fear of what others will say? *Lord, I need help to stay on top of my world, but I am hesitant to do that for a number of reasons. I can't really afford it, but I also can't afford **not** to expand the people in my world to organize my day and life. Help me to confront my fears and then show me who I can get to help me, even if I must pay them.*

April 27
Write It Down

"Write down the revelation and make it plain on tablets so that a herald may run with it. For the revelation awaits an appointed time; it speaks of the end and will not prove false. Though it linger, wait for it; it will certainly come and will not delay"
- Habakkuk 2:2-3.

You saw this passage last month when we studied time management but it warrants repeating for organization. When you have a thought, a creative idea, a project to do, or anything else, you need a place to write it down.

That place needs to have some system to it so you can retrieve it and add or take away items as the need arises - and it can be paper or electronic. **Where do you record your thoughts or keep your goals and daily to do list? Do you carry it with you everywhere? Is it organized in such a way that you can recall things easily?** *Lord, I rely far too much on my memory. I need discipline to write things down and some type of organization to be able to find those things when I need them. Help me to find and build a time management system that works for me and then teach me how to use it so that I can reach the maximum level of efficiency possible in my life.*

April 28
Promotion

"Whoever can be trusted with very little can also be trusted with much, and whoever is dishonest with very little will also be dishonest with much"
- Luke 16:10.

Organization may seem insignificant and unimportant, but if it is, that makes it all the more important to master. Today's verse indicates that your faithfulness over little things determines your ability to handle larger, weightier duties and responsibilities. God uses those smaller things to train and discipline you for more. **Are you being faithful with the little with which you have been entrusted? Can you accept the reality that the little is your preparation for the more? What changes should you make to embrace this concept?** *Lord, I have not been faithful with the little, at times thinking it not worthy of my attention while I wait for promotion or more responsibility. I see now I was wrong. I determine today, with Your help, to be faithful to organize my world, seeing it as my schooling for greater things.*

April 29
Worldly Wealth

"So if you have not been trustworthy in handling worldly wealth, who will trust you with true riches?"
- Luke 16:11.

How you handle money indicates how you will handle true riches, which are ministry opportunities to change lives and impact communities. Handling true riches means you are paying bills on time, saving when possible, and being generous with those in need. That requires discipline to move beyond good intentions to actual performance. **How faithful are you with money? Do you see how it is training for true riches? Where can you improve?** *Lord, You have entrusted me with some worldly wealth and You are watching how I handle it. That will determine what else You give me to do. Help me to organize my financial world with excellence, not as an end, but as a means to an end - the end being serving You in more significant ways in the future.*

April 30
Stewardship

"And if you have not been trustworthy with someone else's property, who will give you property of your own?" - Luke 16:12.

God is watching how you treat that which belongs to another, which is called stewardship. That stewardship may be at work or in your personal life, for how you treat the things of others will determine how quickly God gives you your own. **Do you borrow things and not return them? Is your workspace a mess? Do you lose things at work, or have you neglected to organize your work area so you can maximize your efficiency and effectiveness for your employers? Have you given any thought to how you will organize your work team and projects?** *Lord, I have been lax with those things that belonged to another while I long for my own. Today I see that You won't give me my own until I am a good steward over those things that are not mine! Forgive me for my attitude concerning the possessions of others. From this point, I will treat them like my own.*

May

Gold Mine Principle 5

Faith

May 1
Faith

"... and everything that does not come from faith is sin" - Romans 14:23.

You can search for purpose, set goals, manage time and organize your world, but unless you do it all in faith, it is all an exercise in futility. Faith is the only way to please God, as you will see this month. That being said, the Gold Mine Principles only have meaning when faith is exercised and rewarded. This month you will look at how you can involve and increase your faith on a daily basis in order to increase your reward. **As we begin, what are you believing the Lord for in regards to the other Gold Mine Principles? Are you trusting Him for time? Setting lofty goals? Organizing in faith? Thanking Him for your purpose whether or not you know what it is?** *Lord, I trust You, but I know You want me to increase my faith and trust You even more for bigger and better things. I cannot rely on my own insight and strength to be a person of purpose; that only happens with Your help. So help me increase my faith this month to find ways to express it on a daily basis.*

May 2
Pleasing God

"And without faith it is impossible to please God, because anyone who comes to him must believe that he exists and that he rewards those who earnestly seek him" - Hebrews 11:6.

Without faith it is **im**possible to please God, so that means with faith it is ***possible*** to please Him. You have the ability to bring pleasure to God's heart when you put your hand in His, so to speak, and say, "I trust You." Yet that trust must find expression in your everyday life as you act on Your faith. **What are your faith projects at this point in time? For what are you believing God that, if He does not act on your behalf, you will look foolish? How can you apply faith to the other four Gold Mine Principles of purpose, goals, time and organization?** *Lord, it makes me happy to think that I can bring You pleasure by trusting You. Yet I don't want to go too far, which often causes me not to go far enough in acting out my trust. I determine today to renew my faith projects or adopt some new ones in which I need Your miraculous power and intervention.*

May 3
Seeking God

"And without faith it is impossible to please God, because anyone who comes to him must believe that he exists and that he rewards those who earnestly seek him" - Hebrews 11:6.

God rewards those who seek Him, and that includes you! It may take time and effort on your part, but God will ultimately reward you with His presence. You can seek Him for insight and wisdom into your purpose, set and pursue goals, trust Him for time, and have faith to organize your stuff, life and work, but without faith, you won't achieve any of those end results. **How earnest are you in pursuing your life's work? What price are you willing to pay to achieve your goals and manage your life? Do you believe God can and will help you with all these things?** *Lord, I believe You exist, but now it is time I apply that faith to other parts of life, including my purpose and how I order my life to find and fulfill it. I trust that I do have a purpose and You will reward me to* find it as I seek You. I also trust You for the rewards of wisdom for goals and time because I have asked in faith.

May 4
The Future

"And let us run with perseverance the race marked out for us, fixing our eyes on Jesus, the pioneer and perfecter of faith" **- Hebrews 12:1b-2.**

Faith always transports you to the realm of the unseen, but it also affects what can be seen. Here you are urged to fix your eyes on Jesus, whom you cannot see, so you can run the race set before you, which of course you can see. What you cannot see involves what many call 'vision.' **What is your vision for your life and future? Where is your focus? On what you don't have or what you could have? On what you want to be or what you currently are?** *Lord, I confess that I tend to focus on what I can see, which is often what I don't have or how bad things are. The only thing to combat that tendency is vision of what lies ahead for me. When I focus on vision, I partner with You to make it happen. That is how I want to run my life from this point forward.*

May 5
Tomorrow

"Now faith is confidence in what we hope for and assurance about what we do not see" **- Hebrews 11:1**

As stated yesterday, faith takes you to the realm of the unseen. You can see tomorrow so clearly it looks as if it is today, and you act like and prepare for that tomorrow like it is already here. For example, you 'see' yourself speaking tomorrow, but it's so clear today that you take a class, prepare a message or tell someone that you are a speaker - that's assurance of what you do not yet see in the natural, but see through faith. **What do you see? What difference does what you see about tomorrow make in your today?** *Lord, show me my tomorrow and let me structure my todays according to that vision for the future. I want to learn how to live in that faith picture, not ignoring today's reality, but choosing to have confidence in the tomorrow of my vision.*

May 6
The Unseen

"By faith we understand that the universe was formed at God's command, so that what is seen was not made out of what was visible" - Hebrews 11:3.

The reality in this verse is the very reason that faith is one of the five Gold Mine Principles. You don't start pursuing purpose, setting goals or managing time by starting with the obvious, which is what you can see. You start with the unseen, which is God's perspective and attach your faith to that. So, you can thank God for your purpose, *before* you know it. You can thank God for your goals before you set them and achieve them. **What role is faith playing in your personal development and growth? Are you starting with the seen or the unseen? Are you planning according to what you have now or what you will have when you reach your goal?** *Lord, I am working and planning according to what I know instead of what You know. This has caused me to set low goals and not launch out in purpose until I have all the answers to my satisfaction. This is limiting my effectiveness for You. I want to think and plan in faith today so I can reap a harvest tomorrow!*

May 7
An Offering

"By faith Abel brought God a better offering than Cain did" - Hebrews 11:4.

You will distinguish yourself in God's service, not by being smarter or more gifted - those things are beyond your control. What will set you apart, however, is your faith and how you apply it to your life's work. Abel applied faith to his offering, while Cain functioned in his own strength and understanding and you see the results. The same will be true for you. **Where is faith involved in your purpose? Are you setting goals beyond what you consider to be your capabilities? Are you organizing now for a future that is busier and more productive?** *Lord, I want to bring a better sacrifice to You, just like Abel did. That means I must apply faith to all I do. I thank You for my purpose. I want to flow in the fullness of who You created me to be. I want to build an ark in faith for the future, just like Noah did, by organizing my time and my life well. Help me, I pray!*

May 8
Future Provision

"By faith Noah, when warned about things not yet seen, in holy fear built an ark to save his family" - Hebrews 11:7.

Noah built something in faith before he knew how it would be used. He had never seen rain, so his faith was not in the circumstances or what he knew, but in God's word and promise. That is where your faith should be. **Can you organize your life in faith to learn the language you will need tomorrow? Can you take** the courses today in faith that will prepare you for your world of tomorrow? Can you take faith steps today to start your business that will provide for your family in the years to come? *Lord, You often give me an idea that will yield a return in the future, but only if I have faith today. Help me follow in the steps of Noah who built something that provided for his family in the years to come. In other words, deliver me from the urgencies of today so I can focus in faith on the opportunities of tomorrow.*

May 9
Destination Unknown

"By faith Abraham, when called to go to a place he would later receive as his inheritance, obeyed and went, even though he did not know where he was going" - Hebrews 11:8.

Imagine getting in your vehicle and driving, but not knowing where you were going, only that God would lead and guide you. That is what Abraham did and that is what faith requires you to do. You start 'driving' toward your purpose and aren't sure what it is or how you fulfill it. You set goals but do not know where the provision or resources will come from to complete them. **What is holding you back from the same faith journey Abraham made? Are you on the purpose journey, whose destination is known to God alone? Are your goals a simple jump or a monumental leap from where you are today?** *Lord, I crave a roadmap at least to have an idea where I am going, but sometimes my roadmap is simply listening to and obeying You. Sometimes that causes me not even to get into the car and start the engine! Help me to start driving today toward a destination You will make clear along the way.*

May 10
Faith Heroes

"So that your trust may be in the Lord, I teach you today, even you" - Proverbs 22:19.

You must be taught faith to act out faith. That is why it is important to always be a student, learning from others of faith. What's more, your teachers don't have to be alive, but can have passed on, leaving a legacy of faith for you to study. **Who are your faith heroes? What did they do with their faith? How did their faith impact their life's purpose? What goals did they set? Do you spend time reading and studying? Do you have a few modern faith heroes who are involved in your life and can speak into your life, to help you move beyond your fears?** *Lord, I want to be teachable where faith is concerned and be shown how to walk out my faith in everyday life. Send me faith heroes, both alive and dead, who have something relevant to bring from You to my situation. I want to learn and grow, and I need You to direct my study program.*

May 11
Tents

"He [Abraham] lived in tents, as did Isaac and Jacob, who were heirs with him of the same promise" - Hebrews 11:9b.

Abraham and his family had faith in God and His promises and they organized their lives according to them. That included living in tents rather than in a permanent housing. That is the kind of impact your faith in God should have in your life. **What impact does faith have on your everyday life? Can you explain** decisions made because of your faith? How have you organized your life according to your faith in God's promises for your life?** *Lord, I want my faith to be a daily faith and not just on Sunday. That means I purchase a computer if I am going to be a writer. I set up a studio if I am to be an artist. I learn Swahili if I believe I will be going to East Africa. Help me see the future clearly and help me structure my world today.*

May 12
Blueprint

"For he [Abraham] was looking forward to the city with foundations, whose architect and builder is God" - Hebrews 11:10.

In faith, Abraham was looking forward to a city, the blueprints of which God had given him. You should be looking forward as well, using God's blueprints for you. It's not as if you must do it all, for God is the designer and builder of your future. Your job is to see it in faith and pursue it in faith. **What do you see for your future? Are you pursuing that future today, doing what you know to do to prepare? What is keeping you from taking steps today to prepare for tomorrow?** *Lord, I need to see what You have designed so I can cooperate with Your blueprint. First, show me the blueprint. Then give me the skill and perseverance to follow that plan so that I can help build what You are overseeing as the chief contractor. I want to learn how to build in faith.*

May 13
Sarah

"And by faith even Sarah, who was past childbearing age, was enabled to bear children because she

considered him faithful who had made the promise"
- Hebrews 11:11.

Sarah was past child-bearing age, but she put her trust in the Lord's promise to her family and it came to pass just as the Lord had spoken. She put her faith in the promise and vision of the future and the Lord did His part. The same process with the same results is available to you. First, you must know the promise for the future. Then you do what you can do, trusting that in the fullness of time God will do what only He can do. **What is the vision for your future capabilities? What are you preparing for today that will only take place tomorrow? What will you do today that will bring you one step closer to tomorrow?** *Lord, I want to be like Sarah, with the kind of faith that will increase my capability to do more because You empowered me to do it. Give me a vision of my future purpose, and then an understanding of what I need to do to prepare as I organize and manage my time today and every day.*

May 14
Clarity of Reality

"All these people were still living by faith when they died. They did not receive the things promised; they only saw them and welcomed them from a distance, admitting that they were foreigners and strangers on earth" - Hebrews 11:13.

You may not receive what you have faith for in this lifetime, as happened to those mentioned in today's verse. Yet they saw something and welcomed it as though it already was! That's what faith does - it allows you to see something from tomorrow so clearly today that you can thank God for it and enjoy it now. **What do**

you see? Are you basing your life's work on what you can see or what is yet to come? Are you willing to die in faith rather than live in fear or presumption?
Lord, I want clarity of reality, not of what is today but what will be tomorrow. Once I see it, I need help to take steps to make it so, even if it means I give my life to it and it's not yet finished. At that point, I can die in faith, entrusting my work into Your hands and watchful care.

May 15
Today

"In the same way, faith by itself, if it is not accompanied by action, is dead" - James 2:17.

Faith is not just what you believe, it is what you do with what you believe. Faith is seen and proved by your actions; what you do and in some sense by what you don't. There is always something you can do with your faith. You can take a trip, write a letter, make a call, or read a book, all because you have faith that something is going to happen tomorrow. Therefore you choose to do something about that tomorrow today. **What impact is your faith in God having on your vision of tomorrow? What impact is that vision having on today? What can you do right now because you have faith?** *Lord, I trust You, and I know this trust must find practical expressions in my everyday life. Open my eyes to the today portion of every day, so that I may please You by acting out my faith right here, right now.*

May 16
Current Reality

"Without weakening in his faith, he faced the fact that his body was as good as dead—since he was

about a hundred years old—and that Sarah's womb was also dead" - Romans 4:19.

Faith does not require that you ignore the current facts or reality of your situation. It does require that you not base your actions, your words or your future on those facts. As bad as your current situation may be, you are just one phone call, meeting or email away from where you are now to where God has promised you will be! **Can you live in the tension of God's promise for the future and your current reality? Can you live in the promise of prosperity when you are broke? Can you live in your future purpose when you are stuck in a job you hate?** *Lord, I look at my current reality and I could be depressed, but I refuse. Instead I choose to remain strong in faith and trust You and Your promises to me. In my finances, job prospects, and relationships, I am as good as dead (just like Abraham was) but my faith in You is strong. I choose to trust You today.*

May 17
Fully Persuaded

"Yet he did not waver through unbelief regarding the promise of God, but was strengthened in his faith and gave glory to God, being fully persuaded that God had power to do what he had promised"
- Romans 4:20-21.

When Abraham beheld the reality of his age and childlessness, he did not ignore the truth. He simply chose to focus on another truth - God's promise. When he did that, he was strengthened in his faith and gave God glory. What's more, he was 'fully persuaded' God would come through. **Are you persuaded of God's ability to provide, even though you lack right now?**

Do you look at your current reality and come away stronger in faith? Do you base decisions on what you can see or what God has put in your heart about the future? Lord, You have the power to do anything. I know that. There are things in my heart to be and do, but I seem far away from them right now. I choose to trust You, realizing that a breakthrough may be near.

May 18
Faith Words

"It is written: 'I believed; therefore I have spoken.' Since we have that same spirit of faith, we also believe and therefore speak . . . ." - 2 Corinthians 4:13.

What you believe should affect what you say and confess. This is consistent with what you learned the other day: faith without action is dead. If nothing else, your heart faith should produce faith words that speak of what will be as though it already is. **Can you speak of your purpose in 'now' terms? Can you set goals and thank God for their completion? Can you trust God for time and then act like you are, not speaking anxiety but confidence in your ability to get things done with the time you have?** *Lord, I do believe, but sometimes my words betray my doubts. I am afraid to verbalize my faith at times so I will not be disappointed or embarrassed if things don't work out. What's more, even my silence can indicate my fearful heart. Help me to be a person of faith who speaks words of faith.*

May 19
Lifestyle

"For we live by faith, not by sight"
- 2 Corinthians 5:7.

Faith is not an event or expressed in times of dire need. Faith is a lifestyle! It is something you live in, like a goldfish lives in its water every day. Faith is not a parachute you deploy when falling. It is the currency with which you make transactions with God. As today's verse states, you live by faith every day and in every way. **Is faith your lifestyle? Or do you pretty much trust yourself and your way of life, moving into faith only on special occasions?** *Lord, I don't want to move in and out of faith any longer. I want to stay and live there, when I work, in my relationships, in my giving and when I express my spiritual gifts in ministry. That means I will need to learn to walk by faith and not by sight in all things. Help me as I commit to walk in faith as a lifestyle.*

May 20
Unfaith

"People who say such things show that they are looking for a country of their own" **- Hebrews 11:14.**

As you saw yesterday, your faith should impact what you say and the words you use. Faith is always hopeful and optimistic, but not blind to reality. You can say, "I don't have any money but that will change." When you say, "I never have any money" or "Things always go wrong or badly for me," you are speaking unfaith. In fact, whenever you use "always" when describing your condition, you are speaking unfaith, for just one phone call or meeting can change that always into a "used to." **Are you optimistic or pessimistic? Do you use "always" when describing a negative situation in your life and world? Are you willing to transition from pessimism to hope?** *Lord, I confess I speak unfaith at times, talking myself into pessimism and a downward spiral of negativity. How things are for me* today is not how they will necessarily be tomorrow when You intervene on my behalf. Forgive my negativity and help change from a pessimist to a carrier of hope.

May 21
Do Faith

"But someone will say, 'You have faith; I have deeds.' Show me your faith without deeds, and I will show you my faith by my deeds" - James 2:18.

You do not have to choose between having faith and doing something with your faith. It is not either/or. James indicated that he would show the world his faith by what he did, not only by what he said. Talk is cheap and good intentions are noble but both are insufficient unless followed up with faith actions. **Do you talk faith or do faith? What deeds can you point to which indicate your level of faith? What actions are visible signs of your faith? Those can be things like goals, projects, classes or other preparatory works for your future?** *Lord, I want to talk faith, but not just talk, rather do faith. I will take stock today of my faith actions that indicate my faith levels. Then I will adjust my actions to include not only talk but also tangible deeds that represent my faith in You. Help me to increase my faith and my corresponding faith actions.*

May 22
Faith Stories

"Consequently, faith comes from hearing the message, and the message is heard through the word about Christ" - Romans 10:17.

You must feed and build up your faith, and that comes

in part by hearing faith stories and teaching. That is why testimonies are so important, for they build your faith and give you a vision for what you can do in faith. These stories can be from the living or those who have gone on in faith. What's more, you can encourage yourself with your own faith stories, reminding yourself of your past faith ventures to encourage your faith walk today. **Who are your faith heroes? Where do you go to stimulate and encourage your faith? Who are you listening to? Those who are optimistic in faith or pessimistic in doubt?** *Lord, You have been faithful to me, and I take time today to remember instances where I stood in faith and You acted on my behalf. I choose not to shrink back today, but rather to advance in faith, remembering my past and the past of others whose faith you rewarded.*

May 23
Blind and Lame

"On that day David had said, 'Anyone who conquers the Jebusites will have to use the water shaft to reach those 'lame and blind' who are David's enemies.' That is why they say, 'The 'blind and lame' will not enter the palace'" - 2 Samuel 5:8.

This verse makes no sense because later David welcomed a lame descendant of Saul into his royal court. So to what is it referring? The 'blind' who cannot see through eyes of faith and the 'lame' who see but cannot carry out their faith vision are both not welcome in the palace of the King. Read Hebrews 11 and notice that everyone who had faith 'saw' something and 'walked it out' in practical terms. **What do you see in faith? And are you walking toward that vision, or delaying and making excuses of why you cannot do it now?** *Lord, I don't want to be a spectator but a participant in this faith* *journey. I don't want to be counted among the blind or lame when it comes to Your work for me. If I can't see it, show me! If I have seen it and am guilty of delay, then show me the steps I can take today to reach that vision.*

May 24
Faith's Way

"Behold, as for the proud one, His soul is not right within him; But the righteous will live by his faith" - Habakkuk 2:4.

Notice that today's verse, oft quoted in the New Testament, is from the Old Testament. This tells us that faith was God's standard for living in the times before Christ. What's more, notice that the opposite of faith in this verse is not fear or doubt, but rather pride. The proud person says, "I can do it myself," or "I demand answers and an explanation before I will get involved and act." **Are you that proud person described above? Are you disguising your pride as responsibility and a rational approach, when it is nothing more than insisting on having God do things your way and according to your timetable?** *Lord, I see that faith has always been Your requirement for fellowship with You. Nothing has changed, yet at times I want to change the rules by requiring that I see my way before I trust You. That does not please You. I ask Your forgiveness for my pride and I humble myself to do things Your way, which is faith's way.*

May 25
Purpose Vision

"By faith Moses' parents hid him for three months after he was born, because they saw he was

no ordinary child, and they were not afraid of the king's edict" - Hebrews 11:23.

Moses' parents 'saw' something in their son and acted accordingly. **What could they have seen in a little baby?** They saw his purpose! When they saw his purpose, they knew they had to ignore the king's edict to toss the male babies into the river. They did put him in the river in a way; they simply put him in a waterproof basket first! You can only see your purpose (or anyone else's) through the eyes of faith. **What do you see concerning your purpose? That of your spouse or children? Those around you? What difference is what you see making in your life?** *Lord, I want to see purpose in others and myself, just like Moses' parents. Open my eyes to see purpose wherever it is, and then give me purpose vision that will make it clear what I must do to prepare just like Moses' parents did. I know part of that is overcoming the fear that can cripple my efforts.*

May 26
Prayer Certainty

"Therefore I tell you, whatever you ask for in prayer, believe that you have received it, and it will be yours" - Mark 11:24.

These are Jesus' words, and they can be open to all kinds of misapplication. Yet if you wrestle with something in prayer and conclude that God has heard you and approved, then it is as good as given, as good as done. At that point, you shift from petition to thanksgiving, whether or not you have actually seen the answer occur. **Have you ever had an experience where you prayed and gave thanks, even before the answer came? Can you be so certain of something you asked for in faith** that you act like the answer has come, even though it has not appeared? What keeps this dynamic in prayer from happening in your life more often? *Lord, I usually give up in prayer before I am certain that You have heard me and will grant my petition. Thus I seldom walk in the prayer certainty of an answer that is coming but not yet arrived. Help me to understand and incorporate this dynamic in my walk with You.*

May 27
Shrink Back

"But my righteous one will live by faith. And I take no pleasure in the one who shrinks back"
- Hebrews 10:38.

This verse speaks to the fact that you can live a life of faith, but then step away from it, due to the pressures that come when you walk by faith in spite of what you see around you. You have two choices where faith is concerned: live it and please God, or shrink back from it, which obviously does not please Him. **Are you shrinking back in any area? Are you as 'radical' in faith as you once were, or have you 'matured' and become more rational? Why not ask the Lord to show you if you are in a shrink-back posture in your life?** *Lord, walking in faith can challenge everything in me and everything I do. It is easy to abandon the walk of faith by reducing my world to its most comprehensible components. I don't want to shrink back, Lord, but need You to show me if I have. Is my faith walk pleasing you?*

May 28
Backsliding

"But we do not belong to those who shrink back and

are destroyed, but to those who have faith and are saved" - Hebrews 10:39.

When you shrink back in unbelief, it is a form of backsliding, for you are no longer moving forward in the Lord and the work He assigned you to do. You may not be breaking commandments, but you are rendered ineffective where purpose and goals are concerned. **Are you shrinking back in any area of your walk with the Lord? Have you covered your unbelief with excuses? In what area that is important to you are you *not* making progress?** *Lord, I always saw backsliding as doing bad things I know I should not do. Today I see I can backslide by not progressing in a faith area You have called me to work. Forgive me and help me move forward again.*

May 29
Draw Near

"Let us draw near to God with a sincere heart and with the full assurance that faith brings, having our hearts sprinkled to cleanse us from a guilty conscience and having our bodies washed with pure water" - Hebrews 10:22.

The key result in this verse is that faith causes you to draw near to God and that may be its most important result, rather than what you are seeking. When you draw near, you talk to and learn about Him - and yourself. **Are you drawing near to God, getting to know Him better and better? Is your faith journey revealing areas of doubt and fear and are you sincerely confessing those limitations so God can free you from them? Do you know how to seek Him until you have the full assurance He has heard you?** *Lord, I don't want* to pray by simply reciting a list of my wishes and needs. I want to draw near to You and be changed in the process, as I sincerely open my heart to You. Cleanse me and change me, I pray, as I seek my purpose and to be faithful to the good works You have created me to do.

May 30
Pharaoh's Children

"By faith Moses, when he had grown up, refused to be known as the son of Pharaoh's daughter"
- Hebrews 11:24.

When you walk in faith, you are walking in your true identity as the child of God and not a son or daughter of the world. Egypt was the most powerful nation on earth and Pharaoh the most powerful family, but Moses shunned their ways and chose God's. You are wise to do the same, for as we learned at the beginning of this month, with faith it is possible to please God. **Where are you still acting like one of Pharaoh's children? Where do you need to renounce Pharaoh's way and embrace God's, which is faith? What other insights have you had this month in your study of faith, and what changes will you be making because of them?** *Lord, the world system is so glitzy, powerful and alluring, yet I choose to walk in Your 'system,' which is no system, but rather a faith relationship with You. I choose to learn how to walk in faith as one of Your children and I refuse to be identified as a child of Pharaoh's family system.*

May 31
He is Faithful!

"Let us hold unswervingly to the hope we profess, for he who promised is faithful" - Hebrews 10:24.

The definition of swerve is 'to turn aside or be turned aside from a straight course.' When you walk in faith, you must stay straight and true to the path that faith dictates for you. Otherwise you cannot reach your final faith destination. Yet when all is said and done, it is not your faith that wins the day, but the faithfulness of the One in whom you have faith, and that is the Lord Jesus. **Are you on course where faith is concerned, or are you swerving all over the place in doubt and fear? Do you profess a consistent faith or do your words indicate un-faith and un-hope? Is your faith in faith or in the Lord's faithfulness?** *Lord, I thank You for this study of faith over the past month. I confess that I often swerve in my faith walk, usually in response to the circumstances that call forth fear and doubt. I need Your help to walk a straight path where faith and hope are concerned, but I freely confess without a doubt today that You are faithful!*

June

Gold Mine Principle 1

Purpose

June 1
Dabbling

*"Let your eyes look straight ahead;
fix your gaze directly before you" - Proverbs 4:25.*

Purpose requires a singular focus, even if you are employed in something not related to your purpose. The American evangelist Dwight L. Moody said, "This one thing I do, not these many things I dabble in." We can be great dabblers, for it keeps us from being accountable for the one thing we were created to do. **Are you a dabbler? Is your focus singular, or are you distracted with many cares and interests? Where do you invest your energy and creative expression? What can you do to improve your focus?** *Lord, I don't want to be a dabbler, doing a little of this and that, being effective at nothing. I want to know my purpose and then structure my life and world to fulfill it. Give me the courage to say 'no' to the things that are a distraction, even if they are noble and can make me some money.*

June 2
Passive/Aggressive

"Give careful thought to the paths for your feet and be steadfast in all your ways" - Proverbs 4:26.

There is an old proverb that states, "Some people make things happen, some watch them happen and some say, 'What happened?'" Where purpose is concerned, you are to take steps to make things happen, while trusting the Lord to open doors while you try the door knobs. Once you set your purpose path after careful thought, you must be steadfast and not give up. **Are you waiting for things to happen and not being active? Are you** passive when you should be aggressive? Are you discouraged and thus inactive? *Lord, things can take long, where purpose is concerned. Then there is the confusion over when I should act and when I should wait on You to act. Give me clarity of thought as I consider my way and a hearty spirit to endure trials along the way. Help me know my role in the purpose process.*

June 3
Distraction Lane

"Do not turn to the right or the left; keep your foot from evil" - Proverbs 24:7.

Purpose and goals require you to focus on the matters at hand and resist all temptations to wander down distraction lane. Yet, fear will masquerade and present all kinds of options of what you can do, so you can think, "There are so many things I can do, how can I be sure what I should do?" Don't fall for that ploy. Set goals, pursue what you understand your purpose to be, and do something every day to make goals and purpose a reality. **Are you under siege by too many thoughts and creative ideas? Is this paralyzing you, causing you to constantly analyze things and in turn end up doing nothing?** *Lord, I thought I was just overly curious and creative, but today I see that it's fear that keeps me running down distraction lane, preventing me from focusing on the main things in my life. I have a good idea what I must do and today I commit to do something to bring me closer to purpose and goal fulfillment.*

June 4
Your Fingerprint

"The Lord has made everything for its own purpose,

even the wicked for the day of evil"
- Proverbs 16:4 (NAS).

God is a God of purpose and has assigned you something to do only you can do; something for you to be only you can be. Your purpose is sort of like a spiritual fingerprint. It distinguishes you from everyone else so that when you 'touch' something in God's will, you leave a mark that is uniquely yours. What's more, if God wants you to fulfill your purpose - and of course he does - then He must reveal to you what that will is. **Do you know your purpose? Are you doing it, or at least making progress toward its fulfillment? What steps can you take to know or implement your purpose from where you are now?** *Lord, I know You are a God of purpose. Show me my identity and help me recognize my spiritual fingerprint. Then allow me to touch the world and leave my mark according to Your plan and will. I thirst for purpose and You are the only One who can release and empower me to find and fulfill it. Help me, I pray!*

June 5
Purpose Sounds

"Make your ear attentive to wisdom, Incline your heart to understanding . . . ." - Proverbs 2:2.

When you seek purpose, you must be able to both ask God for help and know how to listen for the sounds of purpose. This cannot be a part-time pursuit, but an urgent desire accompanied with a sense of adventure. You must pay attention to your heart, and recognize the glimmers of joy that are always the telltale sign of purpose. **How focused are you on your purpose quest? Half-hearted or all-in? What is your heart telling you today? Where are your sounds of**

purpose-joy that will lead you to knowledge of your purpose? *Lord, I confess I don't know how to listen to the sounds of purpose in my life. That sound is often the echo of joy from certain activities or people when I am around them. Help me not to be afraid of those sounds, but to recognize them for the seismic activity that indicates an earthquake of purpose is near in my life.*

June 6
Hidden Treasure

"For if you cry for discernment, Lift your voice for understanding; If you seek her as silver and search for her as for hidden treasures . . . ." - Proverbs 2:3-4.

If you were guaranteed that there is treasure buried in your backyard, what would you do? Pray about it? Dig one hole and if you didn't find it give up searching? Let's hope not! You would dig and then dig some more, enlist some professional help, and then utilize earth moving equipment until you found it. That's how you should look for purpose. It cannot be a passive endeavor. **What are you doing to find your promised purpose? With whom are you consulting? What are you reading? How fervently are you praying?** *Lord, I have been guilty of waiting for purpose to come to me, instead of embarking on an all-out search like I would for hidden treasure. I see now that the search is part of your plan to help me appreciate purpose when I find it. Forgive me for being passive and help me see all I can do to search.*

June 7
Expectant Listening

"Then you will discern the fear of the Lord and discover the knowledge of God" - Proverbs 2:5.

When you diligently search for purpose (or anything for that matter) like you would for hidden treasure, you will find it. God is not hiding anything, but he does conceal it so that you will search. And when your search is finished, you will appreciate what you have because of the price you paid to find it. You will also be less likely to sell it cheaply because of the price you paid to get it. **Are you seeking the Lord for answers, expecting to hear? What are you doing differently that can give you the results you desire where hearing is concerned? Are you acting on what you hear or waiting for more and more confirmation?** *Lord, I know You want me to do Your will, so I know You will reveal Your will to me if I ask. Your Word clearly states that I will receive if I ask and don't doubt. I am asking You for wisdom today, wisdom for my life and way. I expect to hear an answer today, and I commit to act on that answer without wavering.*

June 8
Enhanced Appreciation

"It is the glory of God to conceal a matter, But the glory of kings is to search out a matter"
- Proverbs 25:2.

As you learned yesterday, God is not teasing you when He requires you to search for purpose. The higher the price you pay, the greater the value it is when you find it. This is called enhanced appreciation, and is part of your preparation to fulfill your purpose, for it will require the same (maybe more) diligence and patience to see purpose expressed as it did to discover it in the first place. **Do you see the value in searching diligently for purpose? Do you understand this is part of the process as you develop your seeking skills? Are you**

ready today to redouble your efforts to find and fulfill your purpose? *Lord, You know what You are doing. If You are concealing purpose from me, it is because I am not ready to see it, or You know I need to develop myself through the seeking process. I submit to this process and commit to enjoy the search, for it will lead to an enhanced appreciation of what I have when I find it.*

June 9
Purpose Team

"He who separates himself seeks his own desire, he quarrels against all sound wisdom"
- Proverbs 18:1 (NAS).

You will usually not find or fulfill your purpose and goals in isolation. Others will help sharpen your focus and see what you can't see for whatever reason. **Who is part of your purpose support group that can help you clarify your purpose and then keep you on track? Among whom are you making your purpose known to bless and serve them? Do you know the purpose of others so that you can complement them as together you serve in some noble task?** *Lord, working with others can be difficult. I suppose that's why You commanded us so often to forgive others. Help me to find a team where I can be myself and allows them to be who You made them to be so together we can see supernatural results in our daily expressions of purpose.*

June 10
Abundance

"Those who work their land will have abundant food, but those who chase fantasies will have their fill of poverty" - Proverbs 28:19.

A fantasy is anything that is not based in reality. When you try to be who you are not, or do what you were never meant to do, you will experience lack. It may be lack of energy, creativity, time and/or money. When you work your land, however, there is always a bumper crop of fruit. **Where are you chasing fantasies? Where and what is your land of greatest fruit and opportunity? If you are experiencing lack right now, could it be because you are not working your God-assigned land?** *Lord, deliver me from fantasies that include who I think You want me to be, who others want me to be, or what my current job or role demands of me to be. I want to be who I am and work my land so that I may experience abundance of joy, fruit and peace. I will stake out and work my personal land today.*

June 11
Personal Investment

"He who gets wisdom loves his own soul; He who keeps understanding will find good" - Proverbs 19:8.

Jesus said you must love your neighbor as yourself. To find purpose, you must believe you are worth purpose. Thus, any low self-esteem hang-ups you have will shortcut the purpose process. What's more, it is in your best interests to find and fulfill your purpose, for God wants to bless you through it. When you don't search or find purpose, you miss the blessing of God and hurt yourself! **Do you invest time and energy in your purpose quest? Do you believe you are worth the investment? Are there any areas in your heart working against your search, like self-hatred, bitterness or low self-esteem?** *Lord, I am worth the investment it takes to find and fulfill purpose. You created me and then redeemed me, paying a high price* *in the process. Since You invested so much in me, now I want to invest in myself, so that You can have a return on Your investment. I will no longer fight the process.*

June 12
Entrustment

"But on the contrary, seeing that I had been entrusted with the gospel to the uncircumcised, just as Peter had been to the circumcised (for He who effectually worked for Peter in his apostleship to the circumcised effectually worked for me also to the Gentiles) . . . ." - Galatians 2:7-9.

Paul knew his purpose and could express it simply and clearly (take the gospel to the uncircumcised). Peter knew his purpose and could do the same (take the gospel to the Jews). Both were so clear and precise that others could describe their purpose as well. Notice also that Paul saw his purpose as an entrustment from the Lord, something to which he had to devote creativity and stewardship. **Are you this clear about your purpose? Do you listen not only for your purpose but for that of others with whom you live and work? And are you being faithful to this divine entrustment?** *Lord, I want and need this kind of clarity in my life. I want to be able to describe my purpose clearly so others can describe it as well. Give me the grace for clarity and then more grace so that I may be a faithful steward of this divine entrustment from You. I want to be a person of purpose!*

June 13
Divine Energy

"But on the contrary, seeing that I had been entrusted with the gospel to the uncircumcised, just

as Peter had been to the circumcised (for He who effectually worked for Peter in his apostleship to the circumcised effectually worked for me also to the Gentiles) . . . ." - Galatians 2:7-9.

You are successful in your purpose because God works as your partner with and through you. The Greek word for 'effectually worked' is the word from which we get our English word 'energy,' You can therefore say that when you work in purpose, you have divine energy, which you can see when you study both Peter's and Paul's lives. **Where do you have divine energy? What can you do that, although you may get fatigued, you always bounce back with enthusiasm and creativity? If you don't have this kind of energy, what kind of changes do you need to make to get and keep it?** *Lord, I want to work with divine energy and that means I must work the purpose You assigned me. I don't want only to be energetic, I also want to be effectively energetic for You. Help me to recognize my purpose by the energy I have for a task and then help me harness that energy for Your work and glory.*

June 14
Short and Sweet

This is he who was spoken of through the prophet Isaiah: "A voice of one calling in the wilderness, 'Prepare the way for the Lord, make straight paths for him'" - Matthew 3:3.

This is the purpose summary for John the Baptist. Notice how short and concise it was: *prepare the way for the Lord.* Also notice that it was a biblical phrase from Isaiah. Your purpose statement should be as short and sweet as that. What's more, you will probably have a Bible verse or passage to go with that statement that further explains your purpose focus. **What is your purpose summary? Do you have a Bible passage to go with it?** If not, don't fret, but use today's lesson to focus your search so you will know what you are looking for, and what it will look like when you find it. *Lord, I crave this kind of simplicity and clarity of purpose for my life. Help me to see it and also give me a biblical context for it so that I may be rooted and grounded in Your will. I know You want me to do Your will, so I thank You in advance for what You will certainly reveal to me.*

June 15
Come to You

This is he who was spoken of through the prophet Isaiah: "A voice of one calling in the wilderness, 'Prepare the way for the Lord, make straight paths for him'" - Matthew 3:3.

Yesterday we saw this purpose statement for John the Baptist. When you think of it, he never had to go looking for purpose; it came looking for him. He went to a remote area to baptize, had a strange outfit and unusual diet and preached a demanding message. Yet all of Israel came to see him, even those who disagreed with his mission. It is the same for you. All you have to do is clarify your purpose and God will bring opportunities. **What situation, need or people always seem to come to you? What does that say about your purpose? How can you make yourself easier to be 'found'?**
Lord, open my eyes to the purpose that has been pursuing me my entire life. I don't want to look past the obvious. I trust You want me not only to find purpose, but fulfill it. Bring opportunities so all I have to do is obey and go with the flow. Thank You for making it that simple!

June 16
Pre-Birth

"Before I formed you in the womb I knew you,
before you were born I set you apart;
I appointed you as a prophet to the nations"
- Jeremiah 1:5.

The Lord assigns your purpose before you are born. It is clear, simple and doesn't change. How you express your purpose will probably change; the essence of who you are and what you do best will not. **Do you have this kind of simplicity and clarity of purpose? What are you doing to get that kind of understanding? What price are you willing to pay to get it?** *Lord, You want me to know and fulfill my purpose. I ask you to show me who I am and what I was created to do. Send people who will help me see, and help me understand how to do it with grace and effectiveness.*

June 17
Anointed

". . . how God anointed Jesus of Nazareth with the Holy Spirit and power, and how he went around doing good and healing all who were under the power of the devil, because God was with him"
- Acts 10:38.

It may be difficult for you to consider yourself 'anointed,' for that seems like a church word used when someone preaches or teaches. Yet you accomplish your purpose the same way Jesus did His, and that is by the anointing or power of the Spirit - no matter how simple or mundane your purpose may be. You are to 'go around' doing good with that anointing, whatever the 'good' is for you. Another way of describing this anointing is that God is with you when you perform your purposeful deeds. **When do you sense God's presence with you? What are you doing when He is with you? How can you do those things more often and effectively than you are now?** *Lord, when I flow in purpose, it is only because You are with me and that enables and empowers me. Now show me where I am to 'go' so that I may do good deeds and help others like Jesus did. I will no longer resist this anointing, but will take Your presence with me in the power of my purpose as often as possible.*

June 18
Looking for You

"When a Samaritan woman came to draw water, Jesus said to her, 'Will you give me a drink?'"
- John 4:7.

Jesus never had to go looking for purpose opportunities; they always came looking for Him. Here He was sitting by a well resting when a needy woman came to draw water at an unusual time of day for that work (she probably chose the hour to avoid other women). Jesus engaged her in conversation and revival broke out in that village before the day was done. It is the same with your purpose; it probably comes looking for you, and you are so accustomed to it that you don't consider it special. **What situation or problem seems to find you, no matter where you are or how many are with you? What kind of people do you seem to encounter and where are they when you do? What do you always seem to have that they need?** *Lord, I understand I can be looking for purpose everywhere except where I should, which is the history and daily activity in my own life! Show me where I am looking past my purpose if*

I don't think what I do and who I am are interesting or important. Help me see me for who I truly am.

June 19
Him-Haw

"Even in the case of lifeless things that make sounds, such as the pipe or harp, how will anyone know what tune is being played unless there is a distinction in the notes? Again, if the trumpet does not sound a clear call, who will get ready for battle?"
- 1 Corinthians 14:7-8.

Purpose can be made difficult to find because you have been conditioned not to talk about yourself. Therefore you him-haw when asked to describe it, using terms like 'maybe,' 'I think,' 'sort of' and 'kind of.' Today's passage indicates you need to make a clear sound about who you are for it to make a difference. There is a big difference in "I think my purpose may be, sort of, you know, to bring joy where there is despair" and "My purpose is to bring joy where there is despair." **Do you struggle to talk about yourself? Do you frame your purpose with tentative or bold words? Are you afraid of this kind of clarity for then you are accountable for who you are?** *Lord, I have thought it was wrong to draw attention to myself by making a clear, strong statement of purpose, but no longer. I want to have a clear, bold statement of who You have made me to be and I will then share that with anyone who will listen, knowing that ultimately the main beneficiary of that clarity is me.*

June 20
HumDrum

"God blessed them and said to them, 'Be fruitful

and increase in number; fill the earth and subdue it. Rule over the fish in the sea and the birds in the sky and over every living creature that moves on the ground'" - Genesis 1:28.

Notice that God blessed Adam by giving him purpose. Your purpose is not drudgery or mere work. It's a blessing that brings joy and significance and that blesses others. What's more, it's your sphere in which you bear fruit that glorifies God. **Have you received your purpose assignment and blessing? Are you bearing fruit or settling for being a nice person? Is your life one of humdrum work or exhilarating assignments?** *Lord, I want the blessing of purpose. I want the kind of clarity that will release me into joyful work and ministry for You, work that will bear abundant fruit that glorifies You and helps others. I refuse to settle for humdrum work but want Your best for me and others, which comes from my joyful engagement.*

June 21
Indispensable Team

"The Lord God said, 'It is not good for the man to be alone. I will make a helper suitable for him'"
- Genesis 2:18.

It is not good to be alone in life, work or ministry for many reasons. One of them is God-imposed limitations. God limited your purpose and gifts so you would learn to rely on others in their purpose to do what you cannot do in yours. This requires that you know your purpose and gifts as well as those of others. **Are you familiar and comfortable with your strengths and limitations? Do you try to do and be it all, or have you learned to rely on others? Who are your indispensable teammates** who complement who you are and what you do? *Lord, I don't always like to rely on others, but I know I need them to fill in the gaps created by my limitations. This is Your idea, for You are glorified when teams walk and work together. Open my eyes to this need and show me my teammates and give us grace to function as one.*

June 22
Doors

"... because a great door for effective work has opened to me, and there are many who oppose me" - 1 Corinthians 16:9.

God wants you to fulfill your purpose more than you do. Therefore He opens 'great' doors for 'effective' service in the area of your purpose. When a door opens, it is important that you do your part and walk through the door, realizing you don't know how long it will remain open. That means that when it closes, you don't try to break it down, but rather move on to the next open door - that is called change. **Where is there an open door for you right now? Are you ignoring it, hoping that another more convenient door will open to you? Are you banging on doors that are closed or no longer open?** *Lord, I sometimes linger when doors open and persist when they close. I need to be more flexible and open to change as I respond to open doors and need to graciously and quickly respond when they close. Help me to recognize the open doors in my life so I can walk, even run, through them to effectiveness.*

June 23
Enemies

"... because a great door for effective work has

opened to me, and there are many who oppose me"
- 1 Corinthians 16:9.

Your opponents in life don't show up until you start to function and flow in purpose. Joseph, David, Daniel and Jesus did not have any enemies until they started their public purpose and then people lined up to oppose and even hate them! If those great purpose heroes had opposition, then you will, too! In fact, your opponents confirm that you are doing something right and haven't missed the Lord or stepped out on your own. **Who is working against your purpose work? Have you allowed them to unnerve you by their criticism? Can you see they are simply indicating you are on the right path?** *Lord, I don't always deal well with opposition, but I see today it is part of my purpose territory. Therefore, I pray for my critics. I will listen to my critics to see what I can learn, but I will not give in to my critics by shrinking back in fear and limiting how I carry out my purpose work.*

June 24
Anointing

"You have loved righteousness and hated wickedness; therefore God, your God, has set you above your companions by anointing you with the oil of joy" - Hebrews 1:9.

The number one indicator of purpose is joy. God gives you joy in what He wants You to do and be, so you will know His will in any given moment. It doesn't make sense that God would create you to enjoy something and then not let you do it! From today's verse you can see that this joy is part of your 'anointing,' for it brings with it the ability to perform beyond your natural capabilities. **Where in life is your greatest joy? Do you see it as an anointing that empowers you to work with effectiveness, thus garnering results for God's glory? Are you fighting or ignoring this joy?** *Lord, there are times I have felt this anointed joy, but haven't always known what to do with it. Today, I understand not to fight it but to surrender to it, for by doing so, I am embracing my purpose. I thank You for making plain to me what I am to do, and I vow to make the most of the opportunities You give me.*

June 25
Cop Out

"I can do all this through him who gives me strength" - Philippians 4:13.

This oft-quoted verse is applied to many situations, but can actually be used as a cop-out! Just because you **can** do something doesn't mean you **will** do it. It just means you have the capability or the potential to do it. So if you can do all in Christ, then it begs the questions: **"What are you doing?" What acts or deeds are you performing right now with supernatural strength from God? What obstacles are you overcoming as you pursue your goals and fulfill purpose? What more can you be doing in the strength that God provides?** In other words, you must put yourself into situations where you trust that this strength will sustain you. It may not show up before you need it. *Lord, I don't want to use Your Word to cop-out of my responsibilities and possibilities, but to help me accept and fulfill them. I have quoted this verse many times, and now I see that it should be my motto and not my escape. Show me where I can do more and I will rely on this truth to see me through.*

June 26
Strength

"I can do all this through him who gives me strength" - Philippians 4:13.

Purpose is essential because it releases God's strength in your life. This is so because your purpose is doing what you love and brings you joy, and Nehemiah told the people, "The joy of the Lord is your strength" (Nehemiah 8:10). So this verse does not mean you can do anything within the universe of possibilities, but rather you can do anything with supernatural strength that God created you to do. **Are you operating in that supernatural strength on a daily basis? Is joy the fuel in your tank that allows you to drive fast and far? Is the joy flowing in your life or are you cut off from that which would release the power of your potential?** *Lord, I desperately want the strength that only You can provide, but I know that cannot come unless I am doing Your will in Your way. One way to know that I am in Your will is to follow the joy in my heart and not try to figure it out. Instead I should flow in joy and let the joy lead and strengthen me. So be it!*

June 27
Your Verse

"He went to Nazareth, where he had been brought up, and on the Sabbath day he went into the synagogue, as was his custom. He stood up to read, and the scroll of the prophet Isaiah was handed to him. Unrolling it, he found the place where it is written: 'The Spirit of the Lord is on me, because he has anointed me to proclaim good news to the poor. He has sent me to proclaim freedom for the

prisoners and recovery of sight for the blind, to set the oppressed free, to proclaim the year of the Lord's favor'" - Luke 4:16-19.

Jesus had a passage of Scripture that defined His purpose and mission. You may say "Well, that was Jesus," but in all probability, you have one too. This verse or passage describes who you are and what you were created to do and, once you find it, can help serve to guide your life decisions and time management. **Have you identified a passage that speaks to who you are? If you haven't found it, then can you list some of your favorite verses to see what if anything they have in common? Are you fulfilling what your passage identifies as your purpose?** *Lord, I want my purpose to be grounded in and directed by Your word. Open my eyes to see where my passage is, and more importantly, give me power to be and do what it describes. I want to be faithful to what the Spirit of the Lord is upon me to do!*

June 28
Nickname

"Joseph, a Levite from Cyprus, whom the apostles called Barnabas (which means 'son of encouragement') . . . ." - Acts 4:36.

Most don't know Barnabas' real name, which was Joseph. Instead, they know him by his nickname, the one the apostles gave him and, of course, that name has stuck forever. You don't get this particular nickname by encouraging every once in a while. He got it because he was consumed with his purpose, which was to encourage anyone within earshot. That is how your purpose should be - not a hobby or part-time activity, but an all-consuming passion that others notice. **What is your all-consuming passion? What would people nickname you in response to what they see you purposefully doing?** *Lord, I thank You for Barnabas' example of being totally devoted to purpose. That is the life I want to live as well. Help me to move beyond dabbling in purpose and allow me to be so clear and focused that others will recognize and know my purpose as well.*

June 29
The Essence

> ". . . [Barnabas] sold a field he owned and brought the money and put it at the apostles' feet"
> - Acts 4:37.

Barnabas was the 'son of encouragement' and everything he did seemed to encourage others - that's how he got his nickname. Here he was giving away a field he owned to others. You may be involved in many activities but those are not your purpose; they are how you express your purpose, which is the essence of who you are, the main effect produced from what you do. **Are you distinguishing between what you do and the essence of who you are? What is the main effect produced from what you do - joy, peace, order, or strength? Can you see that effect as being part or all of your purpose?** *Lord, I can do many things but I want to know my purpose in all those things and the gifts that I have. Make my purpose clear in the midst of all those things so I can know who I am and be true to that as often as possible. Help me distinguish between what I do and who I am!*

June 30
Your Assignment

"I [Jesus] have brought you glory on earth by finishing the work you gave me to do" - John 17:4.

Jesus brought glory to the Father by finishing the work He was assigned to do. In other words, He glorified God by fulfilling His purpose. Paul said the same thing except he termed it 'running the race.' You won't glorify God only by singing, preaching, or holiness, but by righteous acts of purpose that only you can do because it is God's assignment for you to do them. **How will you bring God glory in this lifetime? What is it that is uniquely yours to do? How will you know when you have finished that work?** (Hint on the last question: you will probably go home to be with Jesus!) *Lord, I want to bring You glory and I see today that I will do so by and through my life purpose. I have a work to do that no one else can perform like me, so I need to be busy doing that. Help me focus on my assignment and produce the work that will glorify Your name before men.*

July

Gold Mine Principle 2

Goals

July 1
Personal Bias

"But by the grace of God I am what I am, and his grace to me was not without effect. No, I worked harder than all of them—yet not I, but the grace of God that was with me" - 1 Corinthians 15:10.

By God's grace, you are who you are. That means you don't have to go through massive personality changes for God to use you. Don't invest and direct your creative energy toward changes that God doesn't direct or require, but rather use that creative energy to accomplish what's in your heart. **Where are you trying to make changes that God isn't requiring? Where are you waiting for those changes to occur before you act? How can you overcome any personal bias you have against who you are?** *Lord, there are times I just don't believe You can use me in my current state of confusion or weakness, but today's verse tells me You can! I will stop having higher standards than You do, and will work through the bias I have against my own personality and characteristics.*

July 2
In Vain

"But by the grace of God I am what I am, and his grace to me was not without effect. No, I worked harder than all of them—yet not I, but the grace of God that was with me" - 1 Corinthians 15:10.

Here is how another translation states part of this verse: 'His grace toward me did not prove vain.' This indicates you can receive God's grace in vain. **How?** It can have no effect when you do nothing with or because of it. **And**

what is that you are to do? You are to work hard in your purpose, setting goals to help produce fruit! **Are you working to your full capacity? Are you taking God's grace and doing something with it? What is the main 'effect' of your work in Him?** *Lord, I thank You for your grace and I want to make sure that Your investment of grace is rewarded and not in vain. Show me the work I am to do, and then give me the divine energy I need to get it done. I will not shy away from or shirk my duties, but will engage them joyfully as Your grace deserves.*

July 3
Work

"But by the grace of God I am what I am, and his grace to me was not without effect. No, I worked harder than all of them—yet not I, but the grace of God that was with me" - 1 Corinthians 15:10.

If you want to be a person of purpose who sets lofty goals, then you will work. You may be employed at a job not in line with your purpose, so you must then pursue your interests after work and on weekends. You may be consumed with your purpose and goals, working long hours, yet never burning out. You can't burn out in purpose and goals, for it is God's grace working with and through you, which is why you can do more than you thought possible. **Are you working to your full capacity? Are you afraid of long hours, thinking somehow it is doing more harm than good? Do you sense God's grace working with and through you as you work toward your goals?** *Lord, I want to be used in a great cause that You assign me, and I am not afraid of the hours involved or the stress of the work, for Your grace truly is sufficient for me. Show me my full capacity* and empower me as I pursue that and keep me on track to do only that which Your grace empowers me to do.

July 4
Go for It

"So David arose early in the morning and left the flock with a keeper and took the supplies and went as Jesse had commanded him" - 1 Samuel 17:20.

For the next week we will look at the story of David and Goliath. David did not set out to find Goliath; he was on another assignment when he came to the stalemate going on between Israel and the giant. You can be immersed in everyday life, but suddenly an opportunity arises and your heart tells you to go for it. That is when you set a goal, without worrying whether it is too impetuous, quick or big to achieve. **What have you seen recently that stirred your heart? How can you formulate that inspiration into a goal? Are you paying attention to your heart amidst your regular duties of daily life?** *Lord, I feel I am simply doing what I am to find what it is I am supposed to do, just like David did. Help me have eyes to see when opportunity comes, and help me 'go for it' when I do, without fear of moving too quickly or being presumptuous.*

July 5
Flee

"When all the men of Israel saw the man, they fled from him and were greatly afraid" - 1 Samuel 17:24.

The army of Israel marched out to meet the Philistine army, only to turn right around and go home when they beheld the ominous and intimidating size of Goliath. That is how goals can be. Many in the church see the need to do something about education, poverty or some other need. But when they think of their own insignificance and the size of the problem, they flee. When they run, they use spiritual excuses like, "I'm praying about it" or "It's not the right time." **Do you look at a problem's size or size of the opportunity? Are you afraid but call it something else?** *Lord, I see great needs but I flee in their presence, considering my own inabilities instead of Your great power that can work through me to help and free others. Then I over-spiritualize my fear, placing the reason for my inactivity on You. Forgive my timidity and then help me take on the Goliaths in my life and world.*

July 6
Rewards

"And it will be that the king will enrich the man who kills him with great riches and will give him his daughter and make his father's house [tax]free in Israel" - 1 Samuel 17:25.

David showed up and heard Goliath but then he heard about the rewards for anyone who could take out the giant. The rewards became bigger in David's mind than Goliath, so he set a goal to bring the giant down. That is how your goals should be in your mind - the end result is bigger than any of the obstacles in your way. **What rewards are you seeking? Helping others and changing lives? Enhanced self-esteem and confidence? Financial gain?** *Lord, I have sometimes felt guilty pursuing rewards, but that is how You made me, and those rewards don't have to be selfish or self-seeking. Yet I do have to believe I am worth whatever reward it is that I seek. I want to be like David and apply this lesson to my life where goals are concerned.*

July 7
Obstacles

"Now Eliab his oldest brother heard when he spoke to the men; and Eliab's anger burned against David and he said, 'Why have you come down? And with whom have you left those few sheep in the wilderness? I know your insolence and the wickedness of your heart; for you have come down in order to see the battle'" - 1 Samuel 17:28.

David's oldest brother spoke harshly as David was confirming the reward before he set the goal to take down Goliath. That is how it is with purpose and goals sometimes. Those who know you best may become your greatest obstacles as they try to talk you out of your direction - sometimes out of your own best interests (to protect you from disappointment) and sometimes from envy (they don't want you doing or being more than they). Since they tend to speak to you more freely and because you value their opinion you can listen and be dissuaded or discouraged. **Are those closest to you helping you achieve your goals or are they obstacles to you? What are you prepared to do about that?** *Lord, my highest priority is to please You and not others, even my family. Yet I tend to listen too much to what others have to say about Your will in my life. I ask Your forgiveness for listening to them and vow to listen to You and my heart where goals and purpose are concerned.*

July 8
Fear Rut

"David said to Saul, 'Let no man's heart fail on account of him; *your servant will go and fight with this Philistine*'" - 1 Samuel 17:32.

David was concerned over the affect Goliath had on the people, since he saw them gripped with fear. He went to Saul, the leader in title only who was also fearful, which made David the true leader because he had the courage to set and pursue the goal of taking down the giant. When you set a goal, it is often for the benefit of others who are stuck in their own fear rut. When you set a goal, it also makes you a leader whether or not you have the title, salary or authority of the position. **Where are you willing to act while others are paralyzed with fear? Are you willing to be the leader when no one else is leading? What do you have courage to do?** *Lord, I know what it's like to be in a fear rut and I want to help others escape their own ruts. The best way I can do this is to set a bold goal to help us all escape. I am not afraid of leading whether or not people recognize my leadership or give me the authority or credit. I will set goals for Your glory!*

July 9
An Expert

"Then Saul said to David, 'You are not able to go against this Philistine to fight with him; for you are but a youth while he has been a warrior from his youth'" - 1 Samuel 17:33.

First David faced opposition from his older brother, then he had to deal with opposition from a so-called expert; this time the king who had more experience in battle and war. Saul looked at what he knew and it limited his perspective. This shows that sometimes the lack of the 'truth' can set you free as it did for David in this instance. **Where would an expert opinion tell you not to go where your goals are concerned? Where is your lack of experience actually helping you as you formulate** your action plan? Whose expert voice do you need to consider but not take too seriously?** *Lord, nothing is too difficult for You. If You have commissioned me to do something, then You are all I need. I don't want to be stubborn and not listen to others, but I don't want Your elegant dream for my life to be foiled because of someone's lack of vision or doubt. Set me free from what people think.*

July 10
Go It Alone

"And David said, 'The Lord who delivered me from the paw of the lion and from the paw of the bear, He will deliver me from the hand of this Philistine.' And Saul said to David, 'Go, and may the Lord be with you'" - 1 Samuel 17:37-38.

David knew how to draw on the power of past successes to propel him into new ones. He had faced other giants, so this larger one would just be another testimony when David brought him down. What's more, David had to go it alone, as Saul gave no support or backup, except to give David armor that was two-sizes-too-big. Yet David was not alone. He knew God was with him based on the past and would not fail him. **Do you know how to draw on past successes to encourage you to new ones? Do you have any past success stories? Are you waiting for others to help but realize now that you may have to go it alone?** *Lord, You have brought me this far and I have already faced giants and been victorious in You. These new giants will meet the same end, with Your help. What's more, I have been waiting for others to help me, using that as an excuse for inactivity. I will no longer do that.*

July 11
Excess Success

"He took his stick in his hand and chose for himself five smooth stones from the brook, and put them in the shepherd's bag which he had, even in his pouch, and his sling was in his hand; and he approached the Philistine" - 1 Samuel 17:40.

David's goal was to kill Goliath, but he took five stones with him. Was he prepared just in case he missed? No. It seems Goliath had four brothers and/or sons, so David was ready to exceed his goal and take them all out. He did not plan on missing, for he took one stone for each family member. Now that's faith! **Do you have this same kind of confidence when you set goals? Do you consider that God is able to do abundantly beyond all you can ask or think, so you can actually exceed your goals? What preparations are you making for the excess success?** *Lord, You are a mighty God and I am Your servant. Therefore since I can do all things through Your strength, that relationship makes me a mighty servant! I want to act like this kind of servant and set goals that I will achieve and exceed. From now on, I will pursue and expect excess success where my goals are concerned.*

July 12
Good for Something

"It is by his deeds that a lad distinguishes himself if his conduct is pure and right"
- Proverbs 20:11. (NAS)

It is not holiness alone that will set you apart. It is the deeds you perform out of your foundation and context of holiness and right conduct that complete your sanctification. **And how can you perform well in the midst of your holy living?** You guessed it - set some goals! And if you are going to set them, then set them high, beyond your reach, goals that can only be accomplished with God's help. **What is on your goal list at the present time? Do you need to update that list? Are your goals 'stretch' goals that are just beyond your ability to perform with what you know today?** *Lord, I want to be good for something and not good for nothing! Help me to focus my efforts not only on being holy, but also by 'doing' holy as I set some godly, lofty and faith-filled goals. I know You can do the impossible, and it's time You did it through my efforts.*

July 13
All Talk

"All hard work brings a profit, but mere talk leads only to poverty" - Proverbs 14:23.

Believers are people of the Word, therefore what you say is important. If you are not careful, however, you can talk about what you are going to do and feel like you have done something because you are sincere. Talking is not the same as doing. And, sincerity is not the measure of your effectiveness. **Are you a good talker but poor doer? Have you been tricked into thinking that making a sincere wish will please the Lord and fulfill your purpose? Can you see how goals can keep an all-tal tendency from taking hold in your life?** *Lord, I don't want to be all talk and no do. Deliver me from thinking that, because I have said "One day I will do this" or "I hope to go there some time," I have actually done something. While I know You value sincerity, I don't want sincerity to take the place of bearing fruit for You.*

July 14
Moving and Doing

"... for the Lord will be at your side and will keep your foot from being snared" - Proverbs 3:26.

Your goals get you moving and doing. While you don't know all the obstacles that are ahead, the Lord does. He is at your side and will direct and secure your steps. With that kind of Helper you should be bold and confident as you set goals and step out. **Where have you been tentative and cautious, fearful you would make a wrong step, so in turn you have taken no steps? Are you moving and doing, or tentative and hesitant? What steps can you take today and this week that will move you along the path of your goals?** *Lord, as I reflect on my life, You have always been with me to guide my steps. There is no need for me to be fearful now. I commit to moving and doing without fear or trepidation, knowing that You are right by my side as a partner as I step out to achieve my goals.*

July 15
Thoughts

"Roll your works upon the Lord [commit and trust them wholly to Him; He will cause your thoughts to become agreeable to His will, and] so shall your plans be established and succeed" - Proverbs 16:3 (AMP).

If your heart is to do God's will and you sincerely and diligently seek Him, He will cause your thoughts to align with His will without fail. After all, God is not trying to trick you or lead you off a cliff so you will have a great fall. He wants you to do His will. So it makes sense that He will use the brain He created in you to lead and guide you. And of course your brain is where your thoughts live, so God will use your thoughts to direct you. **What thoughts have you consistently had that you put off because you are not sure they are from the Lord? Can you see today that they may be His way of directing you? What differences will that understanding make in how you set your goals?** *Lord, I confess that I have been afraid of my own thoughts! Instead of seeing You directing them, I have been too cautious, assuming they were a trap and not a source of guidance and direction. Thank You for Your patience and faithfulness as I have ignored Your presence and work in my mind!*

July 16
Kingdom Rule

"Roll your works upon the Lord [commit and trust them wholly to Him; He will cause your thoughts to become agreeable to His will, and] so shall your plans be established and succeed" - Proverbs 16:3 (AMP).

God is not trying to trick you, or entice you to do something that is outside His will for your life. He is working with and through you to extend His kingdom rule in every area of life, including education, the military, entertainment, business, government and of course the Church. He is directing His will through your plans for each and every one of these areas of life, and His involvement will insure your success and fulfillment. **Are you fighting against what is in your heart because it doesn't seem spiritual enough? Do you have a vision for an area of life mentioned above? What goals can you set in those areas that will make a difference for God and the people you will serve?**

Lord, I have ideas, but some don't seem spiritual and I have struggled to know which ones are in line with Your will. Now I see that they all may be! I won't really know until I set a goal and pursue the end result. So from now on, I will relax and trust You, confident my ideas aren't tricks from our enemy, but treasures from my Father.

July 17
Eternity

"And Joseph made the Israelites swear an oath and said, 'God will surely come to your aid, and then you must carry my bones up from this place'"
- Genesis 50:25.

Joseph set a goal that could not be fulfilled in his lifetime: to be buried in the Promised Land and not Egypt.
The good news about working on goals is that when entrusted to the Lord, He can see them completed, even after you're gone. So you can write, compose, build, teach and create today in faith, for the One who lives forever will oversee your work and bring it to completion.
Are you setting goals in faith? Are you willing to work today and entrust God for fulfillment after you're with Him? What effect can this mindset have on your work today? Lord, I like the thought of working today for something that will outlast me, something I may not see fulfilled in my lifetime. That sets me free to work, trusting You for the results. My only job is to be obedient; You will handle the results. From now on, I will work and set goals with eternity in mind and view.

July 18
Your Dreams

"Although Joseph recognized his brothers, they did

not recognize him. Then he remembered his dreams about them and said to them, 'You are spies! You have come to see where our land is unprotected'"
- Genesis 42:8-9.

When Joseph's brothers came to Egypt to buy food, they did not recognize him, but he did them. What's so remarkable is that he had not seen them in 22 years! If you don't remember your dreams from last night, how did Joseph remember his dreams of his brothers bowing down to him for 22 years? He did so because he lived in those dreams, visualizing and pondering them. He used those dreams to sustain him during the dark years of prison and loneliness. **What dream is sustaining you? Have you formulated it into a goal? How long are you prepared to devote yourself to see that dream become a reality?** *Lord, I want to be like Joseph, a man of faith, dreams and goals. Give me a sustaining vision and then help me play a role in making it a reality as I set goals and then pursue those goals, if no place else except in my mind and imagination. Then what is in my mind will pour out into reality at the right time, in the right place.*

July 19
Wandering

"When Joseph arrived at Shechem, a man found him wandering around in the fields and asked him, 'What are you looking for?' He replied, 'I'm looking for my brothers. Can you tell me where they are grazing their flocks?' 'They have moved on from here,' the man answered. 'I heard them say, "Let's go to Dothan"'" - Genesis 37:14b-17.

Joseph left home to look for his brothers, but he was

wandering. Then God sent a mysterious man who put him back on track to find his brothers, who sold him into slavery. That painful event helped Joseph fulfill his dreams of leading his family, but it would not have happened if Joseph had not run into that man.

God is there to help you fulfill your dreams, even when you are wandering and have lost your way. **If someone asks, "What are you looking for?", how would you answer? Are you counting on God's supernatural help, thus setting goals beyond your current capabilities? Are there those who, like the mysterious man, help you when you are wandering?** *Lord, I am counting on Your help, so I am setting lofty goals that require Your supernatural assistance. Send me people like the man in this story to help me when I wander, and then help me trust the direction You provide through those chance encounters.*

July 20
Deadlines

"The Proverbs of Solomon, son of David, king of Israel: for gaining wisdom and instruction; for understanding words of insight . . . ."
- Proverbs 1:1-2.

Solomon's proverbs did not fall from heaven. While inspired of the Spirit, they became a reality because he had a purpose and set a goal to complete the project. He also knew why he was writing and spelled it out in the first verses of the book. Your good and God-inspired ideas won't get done unless you set a goal, which should include a time limit if all goes as you anticipate. **What is in your heart to do? How can you express and structure it into a goal? What deadline you will set?** *Lord, I am grateful for what men and women who have* *gone before me have done for You; I know those things were not accidents. They set goals, trusted You and worked hard. Now it's my turn and I want to set goals with deadlines that will help others and glorify You.*

July 21
Creativity

"These are more proverbs of Solomon, compiled by the men of Hezekiah king of Judah . . . ."
- Proverbs 25:1.

There were men who found Solomon's proverbs and took it upon themselves to compile, edit and publish them in some format. Their creativity was not in producing the proverbs but in preserving them, and it took work. Today we thank God for their diligence. **What project is in your heart, but you are dismissing it because it is not 'creative' enough? Do you think those transcribers set a goal for what they were doing and how they would do it? What goals can you set that will bless others while possibly saving the work of some other creator who doesn't have your organizational or editing skills?** *Lord, my definition of creativity can be limiting at times. These men had a creative idea based on someone else's work and You honored and used it. This sets me free so I can be creative according to my own gifts and experience. Help me be true to who You have made me to be.*

July 22
Long-Term

"In the eleventh year in the month of Bul, the eighth month, the temple was finished in all its details

according to its specifications. He had spent seven years building it" - 1 Kings 6:38.

Solomon built the Temple of the Lord as his father David had directed him to do. When you read the verses before this one, you see how detailed the plans were. We once again see that something great for the Lord did not just happen, but required a lot of goals and plans to go along with them. What's more, the job wasn't finished in a day, but took seven years! That's a long-term goal for sure. **What are your long-term goals? How long are you prepared to work on something to see it come to pass? What plans do you have to go along with your goals, or are you simply waiting on the Lord to do what only you can do?** *Lord, I sometimes have a short-term mentality, looking to what I can do in a month or a year. Give me a bigger dream that will require bigger goals and will necessitate bigger plans and take a longer time. I want to live for something beyond me that, by Your grace, will still be around after I'm gone.*

July 23
Goals Awry

"It took Solomon thirteen years, however, to complete the construction of his palace"
- 1 Kings 7:1.

Unfortunately, once Solomon had tasted long-term goals and plans, he began to apply the concepts to building his own kingdom. While it took him seven years to build God's house, it took him almost twice as long to build his own house. That's not good, but notice the power and effectiveness of goals still applied, even though his motives were not pure. **Where have you been holding back setting goals because you were afraid they**

may lead you astray? Can you see the answer to that problem is not to stop setting goals, but to work to insure that your goals glorify God and fulfill your purpose? *Lord, Solomon got filled with himself and that eclipsed the brightness of Your presence in his mind and heart. That caused him to take a good thing You created - goals - and turn it into something selfish. Deliver me from that tendency, Lord, and help me use the power of goals and planning as You intended.*

July 24
For Others

"He spoke three thousand proverbs and his songs numbered a thousand and five. He spoke about plant life, from the cedar of Lebanon to the hyssop that grows out of walls. He also spoke about animals and birds, reptiles and fish. From all nations people came to listen to Solomon's wisdom, sent by all the kings of the world, who had heard of his wisdom"
- 1 Kings 4:32-34.

Solomon produced a huge amount of work from his God-given wisdom. That work required effort to produce, maintain and publish. What's more, the world beat a path to Solomon's door to hear him and see what God had done in his life. There are lessons here for you to learn.

Are you preserving your body of life's work? Do you set goals to maximize the amount and quality? Who can access it? What more do you have plans to do? *Lord, I have asked You for wisdom many times, and You have always delivered as promised. Today I see that Your wisdom is not just for me, but for others. Help to value what You give me, and help me preserve and present it in such a way that others can access and be blessed by it as well.*

July 25
Outer Reality

"When the queen of Sheba saw all the wisdom of Solomon and the palace he had built, the food on his table, the seating of his officials, the attending servants in their robes, his cupbearers, and the burnt offerings he made at the temple of the Lord, she was overwhelmed" - 1 Kings 10:4.

The queen of Sheba saw the results of Solomon's wisdom. It was tangible and Solomon worked to organize his kingdom so that what was inside him could find an outside expression. The only way to translate what is inside you is to set a goal so that what you see in faith can eventually be seen by others. What's more, the queen was overwhelmed and praised Solomon's God for what she beheld. **When is the last time someone praised your God for what they saw you produce through Him? What are you doing to transfer your inner vision to outer reality? In other words, what goals are you setting to make your dreams a reality?** *Lord, I want to be a good witness for You and part of that is to make the vision in my heart a reality through goals as I trust in You. I want those who come in contact with me to know that I serve a great and powerful God, so help me set lofty goals worthy of an awesome God, just like Solomon did.*

July 26
Slackness

"One who is slack in his work is brother to one who destroys" - Proverbs 18:9.

If you were to build something and someone destroyed

it, you would see that as a criminal act. Yet if you did **not** build something that was in your heart, you would not see that as criminal. But the end result is the same - in both cases, the world is deprived of something you could have built or done. The point is: Your inability to be productive robs the world of what you have in you that is unique to you, giving you something in common with one who would destroy what another built. **What is the world losing by your inactivity? Where are you excusing your slackness as 'no big deal?' Where do you need a change of attitude to create more urgency and less slackness?** *Lord, I have excused the slackness in my work for a number of reasons, like I am too busy, the time isn't right or I don't have time. Yet I am robbing the world and others of who I am and what it is that only I can do! Help me to see my inactivity and slackness for the sin it truly is so I have incentive to move and act.*

July 27
God's Co-Worker

"As God's co-workers we urge you not to receive God's grace in vain" - 2 Corinthians 6:1.

This verse has two important points. First, you are a co-worker with God. He cannot do certain things if He can't do them through you, and will have to find another co-worker. Second, you are urged **not** to receive God's grace in vain, which means you **can** receive God's grace and not do anything with it by choice. The grace can be wasted by not taking full advantage of God being your co-worker by drawing on His help and power. **Do you see yourself as God's co-worker? How are you wasting God's grace? Are you taking full advantage of the help God, your Co-worker, can provide in**

your partnership? *Lord, I want to be a good co-worker. What's more, I don't want to be guilty of receiving Your grace in vain. Help me to maximize our relationship as I set goals and then count on Your power to help me finish the job. I want to work with You to maximize my impact for You.*

July 28
Power

"I pray that the eyes of your heart may be enlightened in order that you may know the hope to which he has called you, the riches of his glorious inheritance in his holy people, and his incomparably great power for us who believe. That power is the same as the mighty strength he exerted when he raised Christ from the dead and seated him at his right hand in the heavenly realms . . . ."
- Ephesians 1:19-20.

You need God's help to see that you have tremendous power available to you as you carry out your life's purpose and pursue your goals. What kind of power? It is the same power that God exerted when He raised Christ from the dead and then seated Him at His right hand. Now that's power that cannot be stopped and cannot end. Consider the fact that you have the same Spirit living in you who raised Christ from the dead and then go draw on that power to achieve great things for God. **Do your eyes need to be opened? Are you effectively drawing on the power that is yours in Christ? What can you point to that shows this power at work in your life?** *Lord, I am under-living my life, for I have not learned how to make the power in today's passage part of my daily routine. I am sitting on a great generator and I am only drawing enough juice to run a* *hot plate! Open my eyes to realize that power and then help me use that power to do great things for You.*

July 29
Goal Power

"I became a servant of this gospel by the gift of God's grace given me through the working of his power" - Ephesians 3:7.

The word for 'working' here is the Greek word for our English word 'energy.' That is what you need, what you should be looking for, if you want to achieve lofty goals with supernatural results - God's power. This power is available to you when you serve your purpose and it is a gift from God. When you see this truth, you decide to make the most of your purpose by setting goals that take you out of your comfort zone and beyond your natural abilities. **Do you remember a time when this energy flowed through you? What were you doing? Do you sense divine energy working in and through you right now? What goals have you set that require this kind of supernatural power?** *Lord, I need this goal power working in my life, for otherwise my life is mundane and boring. Yet with You, it can be exhilarating! Help me to tap into Your energy through lofty goals that energize me because those goals glorify You and help fulfill Your assigned purpose.*

July 30
Self-Prayer

"I pray that out of his glorious riches he may strengthen you with power through his Spirit in your inner being" - Ephesians 3:16.

Perhaps you have a prayer list that contains noble and worthy prayer requests. Here we see that Paul prayed for others to receive a special empowerment; now pray this for yourself! You cannot achieve your purpose and goals without this kind of energy, so you are wise build yourself up and pray for yourself. **While you pray for others, do you pray for yourself? What do you pray? Are you hesitant to pray that God will build you up and make you strong in His might? What can you accomplish with this power?** *Lord, I pray that out of Your glorious riches You strengthen me with power through Your Holy Spirit in my inner being. I pray that I use this power to set and achieve lofty goals for Your glory to further Your purpose and Kingdom in my part of the world. Amen!*

July 31
Immeasurably More

"Now to him who is able to do immeasurably more than all we ask or imagine, according to his power that is at work within us . . . ." - Ephesians 3:20.

God can do immeasurably more than we can ask or think, but only with the power that works in us. If there is no power, then there is no God-produced immeasurably more. No matter how big your thinking, you cannot think in terms bigger than God. This means that no matter what goal you set, you should expect to exceed whatever you intend to be the end results. **Is there power at work in you that can release God's power? Do you expect to achieve and exceed your goals? Are you thinking big enough for God?** *Lord, I want to see You do more than anyone expected. For that to happen, I know You must use me. I now understand I can limit Your effectiveness and work. Help me see*

July

and remove those areas where I am blocking Your capabilities to do immeasurably more, and then set goals expecting exceedingly abundant results.

August

Gold Mine Principle 3

Time

August 1
Generosity

"You yourselves know that these hands of mine have supplied my own needs and the needs of my companions. In everything I did, I showed you that by this kind of hard work we must help the weak, remembering the words the Lord Jesus himself said: 'It is more blessed to give than to receive.'" - Acts 20:34-35.

Paul had a full-time job and a full-time ministry, so in a sense he worked overtime! Yet both jobs were a labor of love. Because they were purpose-driven, he had faith for time and was able to do more than most men because God was helping him. It's also interesting that Paul used his time management as a source of generosity, paying his own way and that of his team so that others would not be offended or burdened by having to support his needs. **Are you having faith for time? Are you doing more than you or others thought possible because of your faith? Do you use time as a means of generosity, giving it away to help others?** *Lord, I marvel at how much Paul could do, and I want that same dynamic in my life. Help me to do more in the time I have than I could do without Your help, and help me to bless others as I bestow my time on things that matter to them and prompt them to thank You for my help.*

August 2
Focus

"It has always been my ambition to preach the gospel where Christ was not known, so that I would not be building on someone else's foundation" - Romans 15:20.

Paul had values and set goals that determined where and how he would invest his time. In this verse, he indicated he would only minister and work in new venues where no one had already built a work. That kind of clarity will help you make daily decisions that produce focused results. **Do you have that kind of focus? Have you identified your personal values and then set goals to guide your use of time? What more can you do to obtain even more focus and productivity?** *Lord, Paul was a great man who achieved much in a few decades of work and ministry. I want the same kind of results, which means I need the same focus. Help me to know where and how I work best, and help me do what's necessary to stay focused on those areas of my life.*

August 3
Priorities

**"Then Paul and Barnabas answered them boldly: 'We had to speak the word of God to you first. Since you reject it and do not consider yourselves worthy of eternal life, we now turn to the Gentiles'"
- Acts 13:46.**

The key to good time management is not squeezing more events into a limited amount of time, although often you can do more with the time you have. The real key to time management is setting priorities, doing what matters first and allowing things of lesser importance to wait. In today's verse you see that Paul knew what he needed to do and where to go after that task was done. **Do you set priorities on a daily basis, or do you simply give yourself to what seems most urgent or 'screams' the loudest for your attention? Have you even given thought to your priorities, or does everything share equal value, thus paralyzing you**

when you must decide what to do *first*? *Lord, I need help recognizing, setting and keeping my priorities. At times I am paralyzed from fear that I will set the wrong priorities or afraid I don't have enough time for the more important things, thus doing things of lesser importance while the weightier matters languish.*

August 4
The Time of Your Life

"For through wisdom your days will be many, and years will be added to your life" - Proverbs 9:11.

When you apply wisdom, it affects the time you have. Your days are full of meaningful things and will be many and complete. Today's verse states that wisdom will also prolong your life! That must mean you devote the hours of your life to doing the correct things and doing them well, free of the stress that comes from idleness or the nagging doubt that you are wasting time and life. **Do you feel that you are using wisdom where the time of your life is concerned? Are there regrets you need to address now while you still can? Things you need to do that you aren't? Are your days busy and stress free or frenetic and stressful?** *Lord, I want the time of my life to be all that it can. That means I need wisdom in how to invest that time in the midst of conflicting options. Your word says to ask for wisdom when I need it, so I am, trusting that You will give me the insight I need.*

August 5
Build Your World

"By wisdom the Lord laid the earth's foundations, by understanding he set the heavens in place . . . ." - Proverbs 3:19.

If you want to exercise effective time management, you must employ wisdom, which is defined as choosing right actions in the midst of multiple and often conflicting options. The God who created the earth through wisdom is available and willing to impart the wisdom you need, but you must ask and then believe that he is giving it to you. Then you will be able to 'build' your own world by investing your time in what is most important and will yield the greatest long-term results. **Do you ask for wisdom where time is concerned? Are you leaving some things undone in order to embrace the most important things? Are you asking for wisdom and then acting on the Lord's response?** *Lord, I need wisdom for my time, for there are so many things I can do. Your wisdom will direct me to what I should do. Help me build my world through hard work and the wise use of the 24 hours I have every day.*

August 6
Pain to Others

"Like a broken tooth or a lame foot
is reliance on the unfaithful in a time of trouble"
- Proverbs 25:19.

Have you ever had an experience with someone who made a commitment to do something, but then backed out because they didn't manage their time, leaving you in the lurch? Today's verse likens that person to a broken tooth - painful and annoying! You don't want to be that kind of person, so when you make a commitment, make it a priority and keep your word. **Would others say you are faithful where time is concerned? Do you need to make amends for commitments you could not or did not keep? How can you prevent that from happening again?**

Lord, I don't want to be a pain to others, so help me to be a faithful person that others can count on to be on time and on task. I want to be realistic where time is concerned, but I also want to have faith to do more than I thought possible without overcommitting. And give me courage to admit when I fail and ask forgiveness.

August 7
15 Days

"How long will you lie there, you sluggard? When will you get up from your sleep?" - Proverbs 6:9.

The issue of how much sleep you need has been debated and studied by many. There is one way for you to know, and that is to experiment and pay attention to how you feel after various amounts of sleep. One thing is true, however, and that is you function well with a bit less sleep than you get right now. **What could you do with an hour less sleep that you invested in your purpose and goals?** One less hour a day is 30 hours every month and 360 hours a year, which is the equivalent of 15 full days! **What would it mean to have 15 extra days every year?** *Lord, I want You to extend my days, and one way You can do that is for me to get a little less sleep. I am counting on Your energy to help me, along with being activated and motivated by doing something I love in place of that sleep time. Help me figure out the best way for me to function and still be rested.*

August 8
A Few Minutes

"A little sleep, a little slumber, a little folding of the hands to rest—" - Proverbs 6:10.

There is always a temptation to have a few minutes free and do nothing with them. **What can you do with 20 minutes?** If you have a plan and some goals, then in 20 minutes you can: read, write, take a power nap, make a phone call, listen to a 20-minute sermon, take a walk, or call your spouse. Just because you don't have a lot of time doesn't mean you have none. **Are you effectively using the small blocks of time that are available to you? What more can you do with them that is meaningful?** *Lord, I want to learn how to do more with the minutes I have. Help me not to waste so many shorter breaks in my schedule during my day. Give me new vision for the big thing I can do a little at a time with Your help.*

August 9
Time Poverty

"... and poverty will come on you like a thief and scarcity like an armed man" - Proverbs 6:11.

When you waste time, you lose opportunities to produce things that can enrich your life or the lives of others. Wasting time can become a bad habit, so that eventually your life becomes boring and rigid. When that happens, you have shrunk your world to its most manageable components, fearing anything out of the ordinary, yet desperately craving what you are missing. **Is your life lacking energy and excitement? Can you predict today what will happen tomorrow? Is this how you want to live your remaining years?** *Lord, I feel like my life can be so much more than it is, and time is at the center of it. I dream of what I may do in 10 years, but I am stuck in a rut today and don't see any changes for tomorrow. Help me break out of this time poverty that I have created and allowed to take over my life.*

August 10
Just a Minute

"But do not forget this one thing, dear friends: With the Lord a day is like a thousand years, and a thousand years are like a day" - 2 Peter 3:8.

If a day is like a 1,000 years, then an hour is like 46 years and a minute like 9 months! So if the Lord promises to be with you in just a minute, you know His sense of time isn't the same as yours! Yet the opposite is also true: nine months can fly by and seem like a minute. So, something you have put off because you think it will take long can actually be done quickly if you have faith for time. **What have you put off because you don't think you have time to do it, or do it well? Where do you need to trust the Lord for time and begin to do what's in your heart?** *Lord, You are the Lord of time, which does not constrain You like it does me. So just like money or work, I can trust You for time and see You do the miraculous! There are many things I put off because of lack of time, but no more! I will learn to have faith for time and watch You work Your miracles through me!*

August 11
Moving On

"You hate my instruction and cast my words behind you" - Psalm 50:17.

You are probably thinking, "That's not true of me; I would never do that!" Yet if the Lord gave You a word or assignment and you did not act on it, every day you delay means the assignment is that much further behind you. In a sense you would have cast His word behind you by not incorporating it into your daily allotment of time as you move on with life. **Have you cast any of the Lord's words to you behind you? Are you delaying implementing some discipline, act or project? How far in your past is that item? What are you prepared to do about it?** *Lord, the thought of hating your instruction is repulsive, yet that is what I have done by not acting on what You have told me. What's more, I am in danger of forgetting what You have said by not acting on it for so long. Forgive me and help me get it back!*

August 12
Timely Wisdom

". . . and if you look for it as for silver and search for it as for hidden treasure . . . ." - Proverbs 2:4.

The question always remains with what you should do with the time you have. You have seen over the course of these devotionals that you need wisdom to know how to invest your time. You get this wisdom by intense and regular seeking, the same kind of effort you would exert looking for hidden riches. **Are you asking for wisdom where your time is concerned? Are you trusting that God is giving you that wisdom or doubting? Where is your greatest need for this wisdom regarding time?** *Lord, I need Your perspective and wisdom where my time is concerned. My viewpoint is limited, but Yours is not, so I ask for Your insight today that will help me be where I need to be tomorrow. Give me timely wisdom and I promise to follow it faithfully and diligently.*

August 13
Invest in Tomorrow

"Does not wisdom call out? Does not understanding raise her voice?" - Proverbs 8:1.

Wisdom is all around you trying to get your attention; you simply must have a heart to hear and you will have the wisdom you need to discern your priorities for today! That includes wisdom for how to use your time on a daily basis. With so many conflicting options of all the good and valuable things you can do, you need the wisdom that comes from on High to choose the right things. **Do you have faith to hear? Do you trust that God can and will lead you, even in matters of time and priorities? When you ask, do you believe you will receive as James recommended in his epistle?** *Lord, I ask You for wisdom where time management is concerned. I trust You to guide my will and circumstances to let me know what I should be doing. Help me see the long-term as well, so I may wisely invest my today in tomorrow.*

August 14
The Cycle

"... let the wise listen and add to their learning, and let the discerning get guidance . . . ."
- Proverbs 1:5.

Guidance should never be a problem if you are a believer. God wants you to know His, so He must reveal what it is if you are to do it. As you see again, Proverbs urges you to listen for wisdom's ongoing broadcast, so you can learn and make right choices, especially where your daily time management is concerned. If you want to know what to do with your time, then ask and the Lord will impart wisdom to know. **Are you asking for daily wisdom? Are you following up on what you hear? Are you adding to your learning as you face each new day?** *Lord, I suppose there is nothing mysterious about guidance, even down to how to use my time. I ask* in faith and You give the wisdom. I obey, learn and grow, ask again and the cycle continues as You are faithful to give what I need, including direction for the moment.

August 15
Time to Learn About Time

"Walk with the wise and become wise, for a companion of fools suffers harm" - Proverbs 13:20.

There are many books on the market about time management and there are also seminars, webinars and other training sessions available. All these enable you to fulfill the truth and promise in today's verse: If you seek the wisdom of others and 'walk' with them, you yourself will be wise. Perhaps you don't even need a book, for there may be someone in your life who is skilled at time management. Either way, you will benefit if you can learn and be inspired by others who have a proven track record where time management is concerned. **Why not buy a book on time management today? Or call someone you know who is skilled with time, offer to take him or her to lunch and pick his or her brain? What other ideas do you have to become wise where time is concerned?** *Lord, it's time I humbled myself and took some time to learn about time from others. I have put this off because I did not want it, feeling like it would make me accountable to do more, and I already have enough to do! Now I realize I need greater skill in this area, and there are plenty of folks who can help me.*

August 16
Big Tasks

"I want you to swear by the Lord, the God of heaven and the God of earth, that you will not get a wife for my son from the daughters of the Canaanites, among whom I am living, but will go to my country and my own relatives and get a wife for my son Isaac" - Genesis 24:3-4.

Abraham gave his servant a huge and seemingly impossible task: Go to a foreign country and identify a wife for Isaac, his son. That could take years if the servant was to search, interview and select. As you will see tomorrow, the servant had great faith, and this daunting task was achieved quickly and efficiently. **What large job or project have you not accepted because you think it's too big and you don't know where to start? Where are you missing a great opportunity from the Lord because you don't have faith for time, or faith for knowing how to start or structure the job itself?** *Lord, I want to be like Abraham's servant. I want You to give me big assignments, and I want to have faith to discover how to get them done with Your help. Help me to overcome my hesitation and fear, recognize opportunities and dive in to something big.*

August 17
Most Trusted Servant

"Then he prayed, 'Lord, God of my master Abraham, make me successful today, and show kindness to my master Abraham. See, I am standing beside this spring, and the daughters of the townspeople are coming out to draw water. May it be that when I say to a young woman, 'Please let down your jar that I may have a drink,' and she says, 'Drink, and I'll water your camels too'—let her be the one you have chosen for your servant Isaac. By this I will know that you have shown kindness to my master'"
- Genesis 24:12-14.

When Abraham's servant was faced with a seemingly impossible task that could have taken a long time to complete, he had faith and prayed. He asked God for supernatural help and God answered. Rather than having to search through every woman in the region, the servant found the right woman on the first attempt! No wonder he was Abraham's most trusted servant. **What task have you put off or avoided because you thought it impossible or would take too much time? How and where do you need to have the faith that this servant had?** Be ready to give a testimony when God acts on your behalf just like He did in this story! *Lord, today's verses contain a wonderful story of a faithful servant blessing his master. I want to be that same kind of faithful servant blessing You, my Master! Show me something I have ignored or avoided and I promise to exert the same faith toward getting it done that Abraham's servant did in this story.*

August 18
Your Company

"... lest strangers feast on your wealth and your toil enrich the house of another" - Proverbs 5:10.

If you are like most people, you will spend much of your time working, and often you will work for someone else's company. If you exert all your time and energy there, you will have no time for yourself, your family or your ministry. If you do this for many years you will eventually abandon everything to the company and you will have enriched others, who often only paid you a gratuity or a 'tip' for your service. **Where is the best of your time and energy invested? Are you getting a fair return on your investment? Are you happy there or is it time to face reality that you are stressed, underpaid and**

overworked? *Lord, my work at my company is not my source of provision; You are. While I want to be a good worker, as You require, I don't want to give all my time to a company that may or may not appreciate what I do and give. Help me get my life back so I can have time for other things and interests and all of what you want me to commit myself to.*

August 19
God's Curse

"For forty years—one year for each of the forty days you explored the land—you will suffer for your sins and know what it is like to have me against you"
- Numbers 14:34

When Israel sinned, God contrived a punishment that he knew would impress upon them the seriousness of what they had done - God relegated them to waste time for 40 years. The Lord still took care of them, but He imposed on them a boredom and irrelevance that lasted four decades. **Can you imagine what those 40 years must have been like?** Well, maybe you do, for if you have ever wasted long periods of time in your life you know the sense of irretrievable loss that you experience. **Are you guilty of wasting time? Have you wasted years talking about what you would do, or perhaps tried to avoid what you were supposed to do? Are you ready to stop this tragic waste and take steps to be productive?** *Lord, I can see that when You curse or punish someone, You assign them to waste long periods of time. That shows how seriously You view wasting time, my most precious resource. Forgive me for all of the time I have wasted. I ask You to help me have a new mindset where time and Your expectations for it are of greatest concern.*

August 20
Wander

"The Lord's anger burned against Israel and he made them wander in the wilderness forty years, until the whole generation of those who had done evil in his sight was gone" - Numbers 32:13.

Your existence on earth is to be more than just grazing, breeding, working and an occasional vacation. Your purpose is to be more than not getting into trouble. God has something for you to do that only you can do, but if you don't find it or want it, then you will wander through life. Israel wandered through the wilderness, completing her time on earth with no purpose or meaning. **What are you here to do? Are you doing it, or are you putting it off until a more convenient time, like retirement or some other nebulous day in your future? Are you engaged or just coasting?** *Lord, I sense I am here for more than what I am presently doing. Don't let me wander like Israel did, but deliver me from myself into the purpose you have designed for me. My vision at times is too small, so help me enlarge my scope of what life is about. Then grant me grace and assistance to walk in that vision.*

August 21
God's Strength

"I can do all this through him who gives me strength" - Philippians 4:13.

If you are like most, you quote this verse from time to time. **If you do, then what are you doing with and through God's strength?** Just because you *can* do something does not mean you *will* do it. It just means you have the potential. **Doesn't it make sense that if you can do all things with God's strength that you should see supernatural results someplace in your life and work? If this is true, can you apply it not only to time management, but also to your goals and purpose?** *Lord, I have often quoted today's verse not as a testimony but as a cop out, passively waiting for Your strength to do something in and through me. I want to learn how to activate this truth to my daily living and that includes my time management. I want Your strength to empower my schedule and work today.*

August 22
More Focus

"Then Jesus entered a house, and again a crowd gathered, so that he and his disciples were not even able to eat" - Mark 3:20.

Jesus knows what it's like to be busy, so busy that you cannot take a meal. Yet Jesus kept His priorities straight in the midst of it all, and for Him the priority was His purpose: to 'seek and save the lost' (Luke 19:10). Jesus put people's needs ahead of food, prayer, leadership development and everything else on His agenda. **Is your purpose so clear that it can direct your daily activities? Do you know your priorities and do you stick to them every day? Do you complain how busy you are, but don't do anything to recapture what is most important in your life and work?** *Lord, my days seem out of control sometimes, yet when I study Your life, You were busy but always productive, always doing what was most important. Help me to have that kind of focus and help me to be flexible enough to care for people while always getting the most important things done every day.*

August 23
Hard Work

"Simon answered, 'Master, we've worked hard all night and haven't caught anything. But because you say so, I will let down the nets'" - Luke 5:5

The fishermen stayed up all night but caught nothing. You can work hard and manage your time well, but the Lord still has to bless your work for it to prosper. **Are you working hard with few results?** Maybe it's time to stop and listen and do what God directs, even if it's something you have already tried. **Do you believe that God can direct your time and activities? Do you trust Him for results or have you put your trust in your ability to manage and work? Can you see that it is not one or the other? It is both: your effort and His blessing?** *Lord, there are some areas in which I have tried and worked and still seen little result. Today I submit those areas to You once again. I ask that You direct my steps and I commit to do whatever You tell me to do, whether or not I have tried it before.*

August 24
All Nighter

"One of those days Jesus went out to a mountainside to pray, and spent the night praying to God. When morning came, He called His disciples to Him and chose twelve of them, whom He also designated apostles . . . ." - Luke 6:12-13.

Jesus had been busy and He had an important decision to make: choosing the 12 apostles. So He pulled an all-nighter, praying instead of sleeping. **Was He able to do that simply because He was God?** No, He prayed all night because prayer was more important than sleep. That indicates the power and role your priorities should have in your time management. **Have you established clear priorities and values? Do you follow them, or are they paper values? Can you think of an example this week where you followed your priorities, just like Jesus did here, in your daily work and walk?** *Lord, I have over-spiritualized my life at times, waiting for You to lead me instead of me making a decision to act based on my values and priorities. Forgive me for abdicating my responsibilities at times and help me to recognize, set and follow my values on a daily basis.*

August 25
Equilibrium

"Then, because so many people were coming and going that they did not even have a chance to eat, he said to them, 'Come with me by yourselves to a quiet place and get some rest.' So they went away by themselves in a boat to a solitary place. But many who saw them leaving recognized them and ran on foot from all the towns and got there ahead of them. When Jesus landed and saw a large crowd, he had compassion on them, because they were like sheep without a shepherd. So he began teaching them many things"
- Mark 6:31-34.

Jesus tried to get away because they were so busy, but when they arrived to their hoped for place of rest, the needs of the people awaited. **What did Jesus do?** He followed His priorities, put His needs aside and taught the people. There is a time for rest, but Jesus put a higher priority on meeting needs and prayer and was willing to lose sleep and miss meals to maintain

His priorities and time management equilibrium when interruptions occurred. **How do you handle interruptions? Do they ruin your day or can you get back on track? Do your established priorities help you when you are faced with the unexpected or the unanticipated?** *Lord, I face interruptions every day and sometimes they ruin my day and what I had planned. First, help me set my priorities so that I stop seeing some things as interruptions but rather as redirections. Then help me get back on task when those inevitable interruptions come.*

August 26
Another Interruption

"Then he said, 'Jesus, remember me when you come into your kingdom.' Jesus answered him, 'Truly I tell you, today you will be with me in paradise'" - Luke 23:42-43.

Let's take one final look at Jesus and how He managed the time and priorities in His life and mission. In these verses, Jesus is hanging on a cross, suffering one of the most agonizing deaths man has ever devised against man. When the thief hanging there made his petition, Jesus could have said, "Excuse me, I'm a little busy dying right now." Instead Jesus granted the man's petition and then proceeded to die. What focus on His priorities! What an example He set for us all. **Are you focused on your mission? How effectively can you put your own needs aside to help others? Do you handle important interruptions well or see them as intrusions?** *Lord, I thank You for Jesus and His example to me. Today's verses show just how focused He was on Your will for His life, even in the midst of personal agony and pain. Give me the same focus and* *help me to produce the same results: People being set free from their own misery through my service.*

August 27
A Long Break

***"I, John, your brother and companion in the suffering and kingdom and patient endurance that are ours in Jesus, was on the island of Patmos because of the word of God and the testimony of Jesus. On the Lord's Day I was in the Spirit . . . ."
- Revelation 1:9-10a.***

John was in exile when he received the revelation from Jesus. Patmos is a beautiful but remote island in the Aegean Sea, and John was there far removed from all church business and distractions. It was there and then that Jesus broke into his world to impart His insight. Sometimes, you have to create a long break, not just an hour or a day, and do nothing in order for your heart and spirit to quiet themselves to receive the Lord's insight and word. **When is the last time you made time for some down time? How long was that? Why don't you do it again? Are you addicted to activity, so much so that you can't break away without feeling empty and guilty?** *Lord, I regularly say I want or need to hear from You, but then provide only a small window of opportunity for You to do so before I am off and running. Help me to make time to hear from You regarding Your word and Your will for my life.*

August 28
A Break in Your Break

"Write, therefore, what you have seen, what is now and what will take place later" - Revelation 1:19.

John was in exile on Patmos, with plenty of time on his hands. Then the Revelation came and he had to stop his 'doing nothing' to write down the Revelation. He could not say, "I'll do this later," or "I'm not done with my vacation." If you are going to write and create, you will have to carve out time to actually produce something, not making excuses that you are tired, out of the mood or not feeling creative (whatever that means). **Are you 'on call' for creativity and the Lord's initiatives, even when you are on a break? Do you see your time as your own or something that God is directing? Do you feel someone owes you a break, or that your 'breaks' are times God will use for His purposes and not just yours?** *Lord, once I get to a break in my schedule, I usually love it and don't want it to end. That break may be the interlude to something else You are doing, however, and I must be willing to stop that break at Your direction. Help me be sensitive even in down times to re-engage and create!*

August 29
Sleepless Nights

"Rather, as servants of God we commend ourselves in every way: in great endurance; in troubles, hardships and distresses; in beatings, imprisonments and riots; in hard work, sleepless nights and hunger" - 2 Corinthians 6:4-5.

At times Paul had to lose sleep in order to respond to or finish the work God had put before Him to do. In other words, he put a higher priority on his work than sleep. Of course there were times he had no choice, like when he was involved in the aborted trip to Rome in Acts 27. While no one likes that tired feeling, it is also a chance to trust God for the energy you need to carry on in that day or season. **Are you willing to lose sleep to finish the jobs God gave you to do, or to meet the needs of others? Can you trust Him for the energy and stamina you need for your work? What could you do with an hour or two less sleep from time to time?** *Lord, I realize that You sometimes require that I work into the night, requiring me to lose sleep. That may mean I need to put the needs of others ahead of my own rest time. I trust You to direct my schedule and I also trust You for the energy I need to do the work, even when my sleep time is less than optimal.*

August 30
Guesswork

"Then the king, with the queen sitting beside him, asked me, 'How long will your journey take, and when will you get back?' It pleased the king to send me; so I set a time" - Nehemiah 2:6.

Nehemiah set a time when he would be finished with the project of rebuilding the walls. He had never been to Jerusalem, did not really know much about building, and had no idea what he was going to find when he got there. How did he know how long it would take? He probably made his best guess and it satisfied the royal couple who asked. You may be facing a similar situation, but are hesitant about making a commitment. So make your best guess, get to work and trust the Lord! **Where are you holding back because you cannot be as precise as you would like? Where would making your best guess as to the time it will take help you get started? Where can you have faith to get it done in even less time than you estimate?** *Lord, Nehemiah made his best guess and it was good enough for the king. Plus it got him started on his way. Deliver me from* *my perfectionist tendencies that keep me bound and don't let me get started. Then give me a Nehemiah-sized goal in which I can invest myself.*

August 31
TimeFaith

"So the wall was completed on the twenty-fifth of Elul, in fifty-two days" - Nehemiah 6:15.

Nehemiah prayed, set a goal, worked hard, had faith, engaged other people, organized their work and withstood opposition. Because God got involved in the project, the work was done in 52 days. You would have to say that Nehemiah managed his time well and got supernatural results in return. The fact that the time frame is mentioned indicates that the accomplishment was remarkable. **Where are you getting the same kind of results in your life and work? If you are not, which part of the process described in the first sentence above is missing? Perhaps you don't have the correct project on which to focus your timefaith?** *Lord, I like that word 'timefaith.' I want to have it and see it work effectively in my life, work and ministry, where I do more with the time I have than anyone thought possible. I thank You for these studies on time and I pray You will help me apply the principles and see results.*

September

Gold Mine Principle 4

Organization

September 1
Keep it Simple

"Above the Horse Gate, the priests made repairs, each in front of his own house" - Nehemiah 3:28.

Nehemiah had a large job to do when he started to rebuild Jerusalem. He had to pay attention to how he was going to organize the work, so he kept it simple. He had everyone build the wall that was just outside his home. At some point, you will also have to address how you are going to organize your work and world if you are going to be effective and efficient. **What can you learn from Nehemiah's example? How can you apply it to your work at hand? Is there any project that you are avoiding because you don't know how to organize to get it done?** *Lord, I have shied away from some projects because I don't think I have the smarts or resources to organize the task. Nehemiah was a cupbearer for the king and he undertook to rebuild a city, and You gave him wisdom how to do it! Give me that same vision and wisdom to do and organize something for You.*

September 2
Flexibility

"So we continued the work with half the men holding spears, from the first light of dawn till the stars came out" - Nehemiah 4:21.

When Nehemiah encountered the threat of force against his work, he contrived a plan so that the workers had some measure of protection. In other words, Nehemiah had to be flexible to meet the demands of new situations as he organized the work. Your being organized does not mean you have to be rigid. Instead, you must be willing to adapt and change as you encounter new opportunities and obstacles. **How flexible are you where organization is concerned? Can you adapt easily, or are you grooved to such an extent that any adjustment causes you stress and angst? What can you do to be more flexible, yet still organized and focused?** *Lord, You know that at times I am inflexible and ready to give up when my plans need to be adjusted and changed. Help me to go with the flow more easily, to adjust and adapt with more grace and ease than I currently do. Help me keep my eye on the end prize so I can endure the detours along the way!*

September 3
Creative Organization

"Not only was the Teacher wise, but he also imparted knowledge to the people. He pondered and searched out and set in order many proverbs" - Ecclesiastes 12:9.

Solomon was a wise teacher, creating many proverbs with the Lord's help. Not only did he create proverbs, but he also created the order in which they were presented - and it took time to do both the creating and the ordering. Don't ever think organization is just 'organizing' - it is an expression of creativity that is just as important as the creative project itself. **Do you see that organization can be an expression of creativity? Where do you have an idea but it is languishing because you don't know how to organize it? Whom can you seek who can help you with this important aspect of your creativity?** *Lord, I learned today that organization is actually creativity! That is a big change in my thinking. I now want to approach the organization of my creative* ideas with equal enthusiasm as I do the actual creativity. Show me the order that makes the most sense for the work I am doing, just as You did for Solomon.

September 4
Proper Perspective

"After all this, when Josiah had set the temple in order, Necho king of Egypt went up to fight at Carchemish on the Euphrates, and Josiah marched out to meet him in battle" - 2 Chronicles 35:20.

King Josiah became king at eight years of age, and reigned for 31 years. He instituted many religious reforms, one of them bringing order back to the practices and personnel at the Temple. Unfortunately, he was needlessly killed in the battle mentioned above. The lesson? Organization is important but is a means to an end. Josiah thought his organization could handle anything, he went into battle ill-equipped and it cost him his life. **Do you think organization is the answer for almost everything, or do you have it in proper perspective? Do you see it as an end or a means to end, to help accomplish God's will and purpose? Are you flexible or rigid where organization is concerned?** *Lord, I want to be more organized, but I know that it is a means to an end, and the end is Your will and not my whims where organization is concerned. Help me be organized but to keep it in proper perspective and not see it as the most important thing.*

September 5
Partners

"Joseph collected all the food produced in those seven years of abundance in Egypt and stored it

***in the cities. In each city he put the food grown in the fields surrounding it"* - Genesis 41:48.**

Joseph did not have the prophetic dreams predicting the next 14 years in Egypt - Pharaoh did. God spoke through leadership but God organized through Joseph. Joseph's role was just as important, for without his plan Egypt didn't know what to do and the world starved. Don't see organization as a sideshow or a luxury; it is essential to the work and plan of God! Organization is an equal partner to creativity, and one without the other is incomplete - creativity alone is chaotic and organization alone is monotonous. **How do you view organization? As a necessary hindrance or an end-all practice? If you are an organizer, where is your creative partner? If you are creative, do you seek or shrink from the organizer?** *Lord, I want organization to have its proper role in my life. I honor it as something You desire, for You are both creative and organized, and being the one does not diminish the other in Your plans. I accept my role and want to play it with excellence and enthusiasm.*

September 6
Means to an End

***"Joseph stored up huge quantities of grain, like the sand of the sea; it was so much that he stopped keeping records because it was beyond measure"* - Genesis 41:49.**

It's interesting that Joseph tried to keep records of how much grain was collected, but he had to stop because there was so much. If Joseph made organization supreme, he would have stopped collecting grain, thus defeating God's purpose for those seven years of plenty. Organization must be tailored to the task at hand, and that may mean less or no organization if it hinders what God is doing at any given point in time. **Can you function with less than perfect or ideal organization? Is organization a means to an end or an end to you? Can you suspend your organizing tendency when the need calls for that to happen or does that make you nervous?** *Lord, I know organization is of You, but I must learn when to organize or to allow wild growth that can be organized later. My organizational strategy must serve Your purpose and not become the purpose, unless that is what's needed at the moment. Help me discern what's right for this season of my life and work.*

September 7
A Team

"Moreover, at Daniel's request the king appointed Shadrach, Meshach and Abednego administrators over the province of Babylon, while Daniel himself remained at the royal court" - Daniel 2:49.

Babylon understood the value of gifted administrators, and Daniel was just that. Part of his gift was to recognize and promote others who were also skilled. No matter how organized you are, you can only do so much, and will need to build a team - if for no other reason than you are mortal and someone needs to carry on the work after you are gone. What's more, the king did not try to organize; he chose the right people and let them do it. **If you are the 'king' in your organization, have you identified and promoted gifted people? If you are an administrator, do you see the value of a team? If so, what have you done to build one?** *Lord, I recognize my limitations. I may be a leader, but I need organizers around me to make things happen. I may be an administrator, but I recognize my need for others to* *help do the work. Give me wisdom to know my gifts and limitations so I can be part of an effective team.*

September 8
Excellence

"At this, the administrators and the satraps tried to find grounds for charges against Daniel in his conduct of government affairs, but they were unable to do so. They could find no corruption in him, because he was trustworthy and neither corrupt nor negligent" - Daniel 6:4.

God used Daniel in Babylon and He still uses him today to impact God's people. Daniel was a righteous man, for there was no corruption as he carried out his duties. Yet it also says he was not 'negligent.' That means he was a good administrator, carrying out his organizational duties with excellence. God does not promote holy people who do sloppy work. He promotes those who have honed their skills and know how to get things done. **Do you want to be promoted? Are you organized as well as righteous, not missing deadlines and creating trust among your co-workers and supervisors? Do you pay attention not only to the skill needed for your job, but also to the way to organize your work?** *Lord, I want to be like Daniel. I want to be known not only for skill in my craft, but also for my trustworthy way that I carry out my job. I also want that trait to carry over to my ministry and family, where I can be counted on to organize my calendar and possessions with excellence.*

September 9
Either/Or

"God called the light "day," and the darkness

he called "night." And there was evening, and there was morning—the first day" - Genesis 1:5.

From the beginning, God was organizing His creativity. When you think of it, God is both creative and organized. We know what day the seasons start, what time the sun will rise, when the full moon will be and can predict the tides down to the minute. When God is creative, it doesn't take away from his organization and vice versa. The implications for you are clear: you don't have to be either/or. Organization will not hinder your creativity and your creativity can be applied to organizational needs! **Have you seen your life as either/or, being either creative or organized but not both? Have you underestimated the importance of your organizational skills or been afraid that structure would harm your creativity? Have you dismissed your creativity because you tend to be more organized?** *Lord, I see You are both creative and organized, so You can help me with both. I have often seen my gift or tendency as either/or, but now I realize that both can function at the same time in my life and not work against one another. I want to explore the aspect I thought I didn't have and develop that trait.*

September 10
Partnership

"God called the dry ground 'land,' and the gathered waters he called 'seas.' And God saw that it was good" - Genesis 1:10.

God loves structure, yet He is the Creator. God declared that not only was His creativity 'good,' but also His organization and structure of that creativity was also 'good.' Thus creativity coupled with organization is 'good.' Creativity without order is chaos; order without creativity is boring and bureaucratic. Together they produce excitement and glorify God. **What is your natural inclination - creativity or organization? Do you try to impose your inclination in every situation? How can you develop the flip side of your strength to be more organized or creative?** *Lord, You are the great Creative Organizer and Organized Creator. I want to be more like You! I know what my strength is, now help me to develop the other part so that I am not all over the place or rigid and inflexible. I want to develop an organized/creative partnership that will enhance my work for You!*

September 11
Fruitfulness

"The land produced vegetation: plants bearing seed according to their kinds and trees bearing fruit with seed in it according to their kinds. And God saw that it was good" - Genesis 1:12.

God's organization was not for organization's sake. It produced fruit that was of benefit to mankind and God declared that it was good. 'Good' organization serves a purpose and contributes to the productivity that God desires to see from His servants. That productivity should always be a blessing and of use to others. **To and for what purpose does your life's organization serve? Is it simply to have an uncluttered kitchen or desk, or is it organization that leads to a blessing for others as you embrace and structure your life's work? In what area do you produce your most significant fruit?** *Lord, I don't want to maintain, I want to increase and advance in my life's work. I see today that You are all about fruit and You organized Your* creation toward that end. Help me to do the same. I don't want to be a neat or clean-freak and call that organized. I want to produce more for Your glory!

September 12
It's Spiritual

"And God has appointed in the church, first apostles, second prophets, third teachers, then miracles, then gifts of healings, helps, administrations, various kinds of tongues" - 1 Corinthians 12:28.

Organization and administration are not modern phenomena, nor are they purely management concepts. As you can see from this verse, they are a spiritual expression. God appoints administrations in the church to bring the order in the midst of creativity that God loves. If God appoints an administrator, then God will anoint an administrator, which makes organization a spiritual exercise and experience. **Do you see your organizational duties as spiritual? Can you see that administration in some settings is spiritual? What are the implications for you and your work when you see organization as God-ordained and supported?** *Lord, I see now that organization is not a necessary management exercise; it's Your idea and can be spiritual. I want to be a spiritual organizer, drawing on Your help and wisdom to do what needs to be done. Help me bring the order You desire to whatever role I play, whether in or outside the Church.*

September 13
Big

"But when you blow an alarm, the camps

that are pitched on the east side shall set out"
- Numbers 10:5.

The Lord gave Moses instructions as to what kind of trumpets were to be used as an alarm system, and then how the tribes were to proceed when the trumpet was blown! This was not a small company of people, but an entire nation, so there had to be order and discipline when the people moved anywhere. Some people are biased against anything 'big' in the church or business, saying that they [and consequently God] are not 'into' numbers. That's not true. God loves big and can organize it through people who have faith for big. **Are you against 'big'? Do you have faith to organize something beyond what you can see in your own life and world? What must you do to develop yourself to organize for big?** *Lord, You are not against big, for big and small are the same to you. Therefore, I ask You for faith for big, especially where organizing big comes in, particulary where Your church is involved. I know You want to see all men saved and Your kingdom spread, so help me play my role in organizing for that purpose.*

September 14
Your Baby

"Now when Moses' father-in-law saw all that he was doing for the people, he said, 'What is this thing that you are doing for the people? Why do you alone sit as judge and all the people stand about you from morning until evening?'"
- Exodus 18:14.

You can become emotionally involved and attached to your work and the way you organize your work, developing blind spots to the weaknesses and flaws in your approach. That is why an outsider's perspective can be valuable, for he or she is someone who is not attached and can be objective. They won't be afraid to speak into what has become your baby. **Can you look at your own work and see where you need to make some changes where organization is concerned? Do you have someone you can ask to look at your world and how it is organized? Can you then listen to and apply their wisdom?** *Lord, I don't want to be working harder, but smarter and with more wisdom. Therefore, I ask that You send someone into my world who can talk to me about my 'baby' - the world of my family, work and ministry - and speak even difficult things that will help me be more effective in the world You have assigned me.*

September 15
Involve Others

"You will surely wear out, both yourself and these people who are with you, for the task is too heavy for you; you cannot do it alone" - Exodus 18:18.

Part of your organizational philosophy must be *not* to do anything you don't have to do, anything you can give or delegate to others. Moses' father-in-law gave him advice to do this and Moses followed through. You may have employees you can do this with, or perhaps you need to delegate within your ministry or even family.

The key is to be ruthless to determine not just with what you will do, but also what you will *no longer* do. **Are you overwhelmed with your work or ministry? Is it time to take a hard look at what you need to stop doing? What steps can you take to get others involved doing things they can do to free you to do what you do best?** *Lord, at times I have not wanted to include others in my work for fear they would not do it* to my standard or because I did not want to train them. I followed the adage, "If you want a job done right, do it yourself." That attitude is wrong if I am going to be effective and organized, so help me release more work to others.

September 16
Stubborn

"So Moses listened to his father-in-law and did all that he had said" - Exodus 18:24.

Change is difficult for everyone. Moses was confronted with his disorganization and he could have sloughed it off thinking that Jethro didn't understand or that Moses was the boss and it was his way or no way. Yet Moses listened and changed, and the results seem to have been favorable. **How open to change are you? Have you kept your same way of working and organizing even though your duties and responsibilities have changed? Do you listen to others or do you stubbornly cling to old ways because you aren't interested in change?** *Lord, I know I can stubbornly resist change, but mask it in a calm that makes it look spiritual! That doesn't allow me to adjust, adapt and consequently grow - all of which also involves change. Help me be more flexible and to listen to input You are sending me through other people.*

September 17
Do it Now

"When they saw that there was much money in the chest, the king's scribe and the high priest came up and tied it in bags and counted the money which was found in the house of the Lord" - 1 Kings 12:10.

It is interesting that the Spirit saw the need to share this basic information with us. There was so much in the house of God that they felt the need to organize it, which was not a complicated matter but was undoubtedly time consuming. Perhaps there is something in your world that needs to be organized, but you have been putting it off as irrelevant or not that important. Obviously from this verse and at that time basic organization was important to the Spirit and God's people. **What have you been putting off that you need to organize today? What do you think the benefit will be of this project to you and others? Can you see that God may not give you any more until you take care of what you have?** *Lord, I admit there are many projects that require my attention but I have put them off. Now I see how important it is to You that I pay attention to the condition of my abundance and organize it. I commit to do what the leaders did in this verse as soon as I possibly can.*

September 18
The Team

"Then Eliakim the son of Hilkiah, who was over the household, and Shebna the scribe and Joah the son of Asaph, the recorder, came to Hezekiah with their clothes torn and told him the words of Rabshakeh"
- 2 Kings 18:37.

Hezekiah had his own trusted organizers, who not only oversaw the palace and the office, but who also had access to him to report good and bad news. The king had built a leadership team and that team kept his world in order. In this case, however, organization was suspended, for the kingdom was under attack and the need changed from normal operations to crisis. What's more, these organizers had names and were not faceless, anonymous contributors. **Do you have a team of organizers with whom you work or minister? Could that be your family? Do they know their duties? Do you? Are you flexible enough to adjust organizationally according to the season and need of the moment?** *Lord, I want to be part of a team that contributes to the success of the team of which I am part. Help me build with wisdom and carry out my part with the same wisdom. Help me also know my team and allow them to know me as well.*

September 19
God's Idea

"Now King Solomon was king over all Israel. These were his officials: Azariah the son of Zadok was the priest; Elihoreph and Ahijah, the sons of Shisha were secretaries; Jehoshaphat the son of Ahilud was the recorder . . . ." - 1 Kings 4:1-3.

When David's administration was described, it took two or three verses. When Solomon's was described, it took an entire chapter! Solomon took the kingdom to another level and he did so through an elaborate organizational scheme that empowered him and his team to build, teach, establish peace and relate to the surrounding nations. What's more, this organization was a product of Solomon's great wisdom, which means it had its source in God Himself! **Do you ask God for organizational wisdom of what and who to put where? Do you see that you can organize big events and teams with God's help? What could you do that's in your heart if you involved others in the process?** *Lord, You included Solomon's organization in Your word because it was important to You and as an example for me. Help me to take principles in that chapter to heart and then* *allow me to draw on Your organizational wisdom and apply it to things in my heart that I would like to do!*

September 20
Good People

"Solomon had twelve deputies over all Israel, who provided for the king and his household; each man had to provide for a month in the year" - 1 Kings 4:7.

Once again, we see Solomon's God-given wisdom helping to organize Israel, this time in having 12 deputies, which of course makes one think of Jesus who appointed 12 apostles. Organization is not just attention to detail and structure, but also the attention to putting the right people in the right place so as to obtain the right results. This includes being in the right place yourself and making sure that others are as well. **Are you functioning and flowing in the right position at the right company? Are you functioning with a team of people, each one hitting on all cylinders to produce good results?** *Lord, it seems that Solomon not only had good structure, he had good people in that structure. I want to be a 'good people' in my current structure and support the other 'good people' around me. Help me to contribute to my organization's health by contributing the results that come doing what You created me to do.*

September 21
Planning

"Then David gave to his son Solomon the plan of the porch of the temple, its buildings, its storehouses, its upper rooms, its inner rooms and the room for the mercy seat" - 1 Chronicles 28:11.

The Temple did not just happen or appear one day. A building that large and elaborate had to be the result of much planning and deliberation. After many meetings and consultations, David had something concrete to hand Solomon, something that was an expression of both creativity and planning. His creativity was the source and his planning the means by which he made his vision a reality. **What could you help produce if you applied yourself to sustained planning and organization? What elaborate plans have you developed for some creative project in your heart?** *Lord, I see planning, which is one expression of organization, throughout the Bible. While You are the source of all good things, I must still diligently apply myself to ensure that my dreams become reality with accuracy and excellence. Give me grace to be true to my creativity by organizing it to the fullest.*

September 22
Neat-nik

". . . and not only this, but he has also been appointed by the churches to travel with us in this gracious work, which is being administered by us for the glory of the Lord Himself, and to show our readiness . . . ." - 2 Corinthians 8:19.

Paul had collected and was organizing the distribution of the gift for Judea in a way that would expedite the distribution and bring glory to God. That is a great summary of why you should organize. It is not just that you can be a 'neat-nik' but rather it is to make your work effective and efficient so that people will glorify God! **What is your motive for organizing your world? Can you see how an organizational style can bring God glory? Is your organization increasing and growing**

as your world grows? *Lord, I want to glorify You in all I do. Therefore, I want the way I organize my tasks and work to reflect Your goodness and love for order and not just to satisfy my 'neat-nik' personal preferences. Help me to do things right, as Paul did, so Your work will be furthered and reflect Your love for those around me.*

September 23
Precautions

**". . . taking precaution so that no one will discredit us in our administration of this generous gift . . . ."
- 2 Corinthians 8:20 (NAS).**

Paul organized the benevolent offering in a special way because it involved money and he knew it would be easy to be accused of mismanagement. Paul knew that disorganization in this case would be painful and bring disrepute to the Lord's work. The more public your work - the more people it touches - the more attention you must pay to detail and organization. **Do you recognize organization as important in the work you do? Are you organized enough to prevent needless controversy where money and people's lives are concerned? Do you take precautions when organizing for the Lord's work?** *Lord, I want to insure that the work I do for You is not discredited due to sloppiness or neglect. Give me wisdom to know when to go the extra mile with organization, taking correct precautions to make sure opportunities from You are not squandered, lost or discredited.*

September 24
Your Signature

". . . and the face-cloth which had been on His

head, not lying with the linen wrappings, but rolled up in a place by itself" - John 20:7.

Jesus did not come back from the dead only to throw off his grave clothes. Instead, he neatly folded his face-cloth and left it where He had been laid. That could have been a personal habit of Jesus, for the disciples recognized this detail when they entered the tomb and were assured that Jesus was alive and had not simply been removed. In other words, Jesus had certain organizing traits that brought comfort and reassurance to others! **What is your organizing signature that others would recognize? Does the fact that Jesus was neat and organized inspire you to be and do the same? Are your organizational habits a blessing to others?** *Lord, I want to have an organizing 'signature,' something that distinguishes my work style from that of others. Help my organizational efforts be consistent with my values and life philosophy so that my habits may be a blessing and comfort to others. And ultimately may my signature bring You glory!*

September 25
Carry Forward

"For you hate discipline, and you cast My words behind you" - Psalm 50:17.

All it takes for you to cast God's word behind you is to get a word, not have a system to maintain it and then to walk away. That 'word' stays behind you no matter how good your intentions, which points out the most important reason you organize your world: To honor and keep before you God's will and purpose for your life. That takes discipline and the will to stay on top of your world, which must include God's input. **Do you have a** promise or word from the Lord that is now far behind you because you did not bring it forward with you? Is your poor organizational skill the problem? What changes do you need to make to bring the word of the Lord with you as you go? *Lord, I don't want to give You second best. I want to organize my world with the priority to carry Your will with me wherever I go. Help me eliminate distractions and give me wisdom to organize on a daily basis for the right reason - which is You.*

September 26
Clutter

"How blessed is the man who does not walk in the counsel of the wicked, nor stand in the path of sinners, nor sit in the seat of scoffers! But his delight is in the law of the Lord, and in His law he meditates day and night" - Psalm 1:1-2.

Here is a definition of organization for you to consider: the removal or ordering of all clutter, whether physical or mental, in order that you may give attention to your highest priorities at any given point in time. If you are going to meditate in God's law day and night, your mind has to be free and clear of clutter, which includes worry, stress from procrastination and anger. **Does your world reflect today's definition? Is your focus on God's word and will or on putting out fires and managing stress from your disorganized world? What can you do to streamline your world to better focus on what's most important?** *Lord, I know my world is too cluttered and that hinders me from serving You. In some sense, I use my disorganization as an excuse not to do certain things, promising myself I will change, but seldom following through. I ask Your forgiveness for when my mess has hindered Your work in my life.*

September 27
More

"Wisdom has built her house, she has hewn out her seven pillars; She has prepared her food, she has mixed her wine; She has also set her table"
- Proverbs 9:1-2.

As stated in this devotional many times, you need more wisdom in your life if you are going to have purpose and build on that purpose. Building requires an orderly plan, just like having a dinner party does. **How do you get wisdom?** You get it by asking the Lord, by listening, by learning from experience and from others and by making some mistakes. Ultimately, it is a gift of God, but He gives this gift so you can do something. That will at require you to organize your life's work and ministry. **What house are you building? What dinner party are you preparing? In other words, what work project are you involved in that requires more insight and wisdom than you have today?** *Lord, today I ask You for wisdom - wisdom to build the house in which my purpose will reside. To get to that point tomorrow, I need more today, more of You, more of Your insight and more of Your love for others. Lord, I suppose I just need **more**!*

September 28
Heavenly Order

"Dominion and awe belong to God; he establishes order in the heights of heaven" - Job 25:2.

When you think of it, heaven is an organized entity. There is rank among the angels, clarity of communication, assignments given, understood and carried out and punctuality (God is always on time).

There is never confusion and everything is in its place and functioning properly. If God values order in heaven, He must also value it here on earth, for the Lord's prayer states, "Your will be done here as it is in heaven." **Does your world reflect the order of heaven? Do you put a high value on this kind of order? Since order is important to God does that make it more so to you?** *Lord, organization must be a spiritual exercise for You carry it out in the heights of heaven! If it's that important to You, then I accept the fact that it's important here in my earthly world. Give me Your vision for the role of order and I vow to carry it out to the best of my ability in the world You have assigned me here.*

September 29
Fitting God In

"Three times a year you are to celebrate a festival to me" - Exodus 23:14.

Israel was not to fit God into their busy schedule. Rather, they were to arrange theirs around God's priorities and make the trip to Jerusalem no matter how inconvenient or costly. That is how your routine should be. You don't fit in church worship service, for instance, but instead schedule your week around church. You don't work God into your professional schedule; you organize your that schedule around God. **Is this perspective correct? Is that possible in today's busy world? What would it cost you to do what is being suggested here? What changes would you have to make?** *Lord, I confess that I have become so busy that I look to fit You into my schedule, whether that's fulfilling my purpose, serving others or contributing my gifts and time in my church. Help me, Lord, to change my perspective and have the courage to rearrange my world.*

September 30
Rhythm

"Then he said to them, 'The Sabbath was made for man, not man for the Sabbath. So the Son of Man is Lord even of the Sabbath'" - Mark 2:27-28.

God directed man to organize work around some time to rest. The Jews made the Sabbath a special day filled with legalistic parameters, but Jesus tried to correct that attitude and received more than a little opposition. The Sabbath was to be a time of rest and a change of pace from the workaday world - along with a time to worship God. That will require you to establish a weekly rhythm to your schedule. **Do you organize your world to include rest? What do you do to refresh? With whom?** *Lord, I don't want to be rigid and inflexible where organizing my life is concerned, but I don't want to be scattered and unfocused either. I need to make worship and rest part of my life's rhythm and that will require me to make and keep my priorities as I structure my life. Help me to have the focus I need.*

October

Gold Mine Principle 5

Faith

October 1
A Little-Faith

"If that is how God clothes the grass of the field, which is here today and tomorrow is thrown into the fire, will he not much more clothe you— you of little faith?" - Matthew 6:30.

God has been in the clothing business since He provided coverings for Adam and Eve to replace their soon-to-be-no-more fig leaf outfits. In other words, God has provided, can and will continue to provide for your basic needs of life. Your fretting and worrying about these essentials does not help God in any way, and in many ways it harms you! **Are you a 'little-faith' as the phrase 'you of little faith' can be translated? Have you put your trust and confidence in God to meet your daily needs or are you working and planning like it all depends on you? And what about your purpose and goals? Are you setting them, trusting God to provide what you need to fulfill them all?** *Lord, I confess that I am a 'little-faith' from time to time, trusting You sometimes but at other times fretting over what I cannot control. I have no reason to act like that since You have adequately provided for me and mine. Forgive me and I take today's lesson from nature and apply it to my own life right now.*

October 2
Impressing Jesus

"When Jesus heard this, he was amazed and said to those following him, 'Truly I tell you, I have not found anyone in Israel with such great faith'" - Matthew 8:10.

Jesus was amazed that he found great faith in a place where faith should have flourished. What's more, the faith did not belong to a Jew but a Gentile! Jesus heard and saw the man's faith, and it made an impression on Him. At times, faith can be lacking in the church and among church folk as well. **If Jesus was looking, would he see faith in your life? How would he recognize it? Do you live in your own faith or off the faith of others? How can you act to increase your faith today?** *Lord, I want to be numbered among the faith-full and not the faith-less. It is my goal that I impress You as this Gentile did by acting out my faith. Forgive me where I have not acted in faith and allow me more opportunities to apply the knowledge I have that You can do anything!*

October 3
Naturally Unnatural

"He replied, 'You of little faith, why are you so afraid?' Then he got up and rebuked the winds and the waves, and it was completely calm"
- Matthew 8:26.

The disciples were in the midst of a storm, they panicked and Jesus rebuked them for what seemed to be a natural human response. That is the crux of the faith matter: fear is a naturally unnatural human response to the unknown and uncontrollable. When their fear got the best of them, Jesus called them 'little-faiths' again because they did not put their trust in God, but rather in their own limited perspective. **Where is fear causing you to freak out in the midst of life storms? Do you see this is an unnatural reaction or as perfectly normal?** If you see it as natural you will not confront and eradicate your fear. If you see it as unnatural you will accept Jesus rebuke and trust more. *Lord, when*

I encounter storms I often panic! I have seen that as perfectly normal or natural, but today I see it as an unnatural response for a believer. I ask forgiveness for when I have been fearful while You were in my boat all along. I choose to focus on You instead of my storms.

October 4
Carry Others

"Some men brought to him a paralyzed man, lying on a mat. When Jesus saw their faith, he said to the man, 'Take heart, son; your sins are forgiven'" - Matthew 9:2.

In this story, it was not the faith of the paralyzed man that made the difference; it was the faith of his friends who brought him. Your faith can and should have an impact on others. What's more, your faith must be something others [and God] see, for it was when Jesus *saw* their faith that He addressed the man, leading to his healing. **Whom do you need to carry through your faith at this time? Can Jesus see your faith? Can others see it? What difference is faith making in your own life?** *Lord, show me who needs my faith! I want to be available to You and others so that my faith for them can move and touch You! I want my faith to make a difference! What's more, these friends acted from their heart - I want to allow my heart to lead with faith as well.*

October 5
Activate

"And he did not do many miracles there because of their lack of faith" - Matthew 13:58.

The people had no expectations that Jesus would do

anything extraordinary for them, and He did just that – nothing extraordinary. Your faith activates and energizes an atmosphere where God can do miraculous things, even where your purpose and goals are concerned.

That is where testimonies come from - when God rises to meet a need that You have created for Him to meet. **Do you have expectancy that God will do something miraculous in your life and world? Are you creating such a need for His power? Where can you activate God's work in your life by your faith?** *Lord, I don't always understand faith and the role it plays to activate You, but I see in this verse that the people had something to do with You **not** meeting their needs. I want to do my part, all the while remembering it's Your grace and not my faith that makes a difference. Help me understand and then activate!*

October 6
Your Waves

"Immediately Jesus reached out his hand and caught him. 'You of little faith,' he said, 'why did you doubt?'" - Matthew 14:31.

Peter went walking on the water as long as he focused on Jesus. When he lost focus and looked at the waves and his circumstances he began to sink. Peter's fear led to doubt and that led to his demise. Yet what a great testimony that Peter even tried and then was successful for a time at matching what Jesus had done. **Where is Jesus beckoning you to step out of the boat? Are you on top of your waves? Are fear and doubt threatening your ability to continue?** *Lord, I see You walking on the water of my circumstances but I'm afraid to join you. Therefore, I sit timidly in the midst of my storm with others who are also afraid. Lord, call me to*

You and help me keep my focus on You and not on the size or power of the waves.

October 7
Boldly

"Then Jesus said to her, 'Woman, you have great faith! Your request is granted.' And her daughter was healed at that moment" - Matthew 15:28.

When you have faith it should make an impact on your prayer life. Here Jesus commended a Gentile woman who asked for her daughter's healing and would not be deterred when Jesus seemed to put her off. She pressed through in faith and impressed Jesus with her faith just like the Gentile military officer did. **What are you asking the Lord for in faith? Are you hesitant to ask or boldly requesting? Are you pressing on even when it seems like God is ignoring or not answering?** Until God says 'no' it's all right for you to keep on asking in faith! *Lord, I want to move You with my faith, not to get You to do what I want, but to make a statement that I trust You in every situation. I vow to make my prayer life more dynamic where I just don't make weak, lukewarm requests, but rather bold petitions to You, the One who can do anything!*

October 8
Growing Faith

"Aware of their discussion, Jesus asked, 'You of little faith, why are you talking among yourselves about having no bread? Do you still not understand? Don't you remember the five loaves for the five thousand, and how many basketfuls you gathered?'" - Matthew 16:8-9.

Your faith should grow by remembering what God has done, then expecting and positioning Him to do more in your life and world of influence. Then share your testimony and look for another opportunity to trust God for more and with less anxiety on your part. **Are you growing in faith? Do you remember what God has done for you or do you need to be reminded? Do you panic with new faith challenges or are you making progress growing your faith?** *Lord, I take time right now to thank You for all that You have done for me. I choose to trust You today, putting aside worry and doubt to say, "I trust You!" What's more, I have faith projects in mind that will require more faith on my part than I have ever exercised. Thank You for this privilege to trust You!*

October 9
Spin

"Then the disciples came to Jesus in private and asked, 'Why couldn't we drive it out?' He replied, 'Because you have so little faith. Truly I tell you, if you have faith as small as a mustard seed, you can say to this mountain, 'Move from here to there,' and it will move. Nothing will be impossible for you'"
- Matthew 17:19-20.

Jesus recognized little and great faith; in the case of the disciples they often fell into the 'little' category. Therefore they regularly could not do certain things that hindered their ministry. **Why aren't you accomplishing more? Can lack of faith be the reason you are not creating, publishing, traveling, going back to school or starting your business?** Don't spin your lack of faith by excusing it as something else. Call it what it is, repent and get about doing the purposeful work God has put before you. *Lord, I confess that I have little faith* but I don't call it that. There are mountains in my world and in some sense I want to keep them there because I am afraid of failure, success, missing you and a host of other fears. I ask Your forgiveness and Your help in moving forward in my faith walk, which is stagnant.

October 10
Doubt Power

"Jesus replied, 'Truly I tell you, if you have faith and do not doubt, not only can you do what was done to the fig tree, but also you can say to this mountain, 'Go, throw yourself into the sea,' and it will be done'" - Matthew 21:21.

Jesus spoke to the fig tree and it withered. He then assured His disciples that if they had faith without doubt they could have the same ability and power. This verse troubles many people, but we cannot escape the fact that Jesus said it and emphasized that He was telling the truth. Perhaps Jesus was urging His listeners to deal with their doubts ruthlessly where God's faithfulness and love are concerned. **What role does doubt play in your life? Does it hold the upper hand or are you dealing with it aggressively and victoriously?** *Lord, I accept these words from You and don't want to misapply them by arrogantly speaking to mountains but rather to root out areas of doubt I have about Your love and goodness. These doubts are holding me back from exercising faith that would please You, so these doubts must go!*

October 11
Fearing Fear

"He said to his disciples, 'Why are you so afraid? Do you still have no faith?'" - Mark 4:40.

It is remarkable how often Jesus confronted the fears of His disciples and pointed out how fear is the opposite and enemy of faith. If Jesus emphasized fear as often as He did, then you would do well to pay attention. Perhaps you should look for fear and not be surprised that it's there, rather knowing that it is so you can learn how, where and when it is holding you back. **Are you aware of fear in your life? If you are not aware of any, does that mean it isn't there? Are you attempting so little in faith that you have nothing of which to be afraid?** *Lord, somehow I think I am underestimating the presence and power of fear in my life. Perhaps I am afraid to hunt for fear since I am afraid I will find it! Consequently fear has a deeper hold on me than I realized. Help me to be aware of my fears and to call it what it is wherever I may discover it working.*

October 12
Amazed

"He was amazed at their lack of faith" - Mark 6:6.

Faith is not something special that only a few have. Jesus was amazed that more people in Israel did not have faith, for He expected they would in abundance. Perhaps the same is true for God's people today. Jesus expects them to have faith with all they know and hear, but maybe He would be surprised again. **What would Jesus say about your faith? Would He be pleased at what you have or amazed you have so little? How would Jesus expect to see your faith operating? What would you be doing?** *Lord, I don't want to amaze You for the wrong reason; one being lack of faith. I have learned from You; now it's time to do what I know to do. I am tired of living as I am, so bring me opportunity and I will walk in God-pleasing faith every day.*

October 13
The Lie

"'Have faith in God,' Jesus answered" - Mark 11:22.

Jesus' answer to your woes is the same as this verse: Have faith in God. When all else goes wrong, when it seems like God is far away, when it seems like serving God is not worth it, when it seems like you have sown and not reaped, when you feel like everyone is against you and no one is standing up for you, have faith in God. When a lying voice whispers that God is not good or faithful or loving, it is all the more reason to have faith. **Are you wavering in your faith in God? Are circumstances ganging up on you so that your faith is weakened? Have you believed a lie that God has not been faithful to you?** *Lord, at times I have believed the lie that You are distant and don't care. I have taken my eyes off You and put them on the circumstances around me and it has caused me to doubt. Forgive me, and today and every day I will choose to do what You commanded: Have faith in God!*

October 14
Answer the Question

"'Where is your faith?' he asked his disciples. In fear and amazement they asked one another, 'Who is this? He commands even the winds and the water, and they obey him'" - Luke 8:25.

That's a good question: **Where is your faith?** The winds and storms seem uncontrollable and threatening to us, but they are under God's control. If God can control the weather He can control anything. So that goes back to Jesus' question: **Where is your faith? Are storms**

raging in your life? Where is your faith? Is your business or ministry struggling? Having a relational problem? Where is your faith? *Lord, You are asking me this question and You want an answer. My answer is that my faith is in You, not in my present circumstances. I choose to put my focus squarely on You and not on things You are allowing to test and prove my faith.*

October 15
Use What You Have Today

"The apostles said to the Lord, 'Increase our faith!'"
- Luke 17:5.

The apostles responded to Jesus' teaching about forgiving their brother seven times a day if needed by asking for more faith. Jesus responded to this request by telling them that faith as small as a mustard seed is enough to get any job done. In other words: use the faith you have and God will work with you. Then you will increase your faith through the testimony of what you accomplished through the little faith you had. **Are you operating in the faith you have or waiting for more? Are you asking for faith when the Lord is requiring obedience? Do you see the way to increase your faith is to use the faith you have?** *Lord, I have been content for too long for You to do what only I can. I have been waiting for You to increase my faith. You have been waiting for me to use the faith I have. You win! I will use my faith today so I can have more tomorrow from the testimony I will receive from today's faith action.*

October 16
Free

"If that is how God clothes the grass of the field,

which is here today, and tomorrow is thrown into the fire, how much more will he clothe you—you of little faith!" - Luke 12:28.

Your preoccupation with money, career and benefits can greatly impact your pursuit of purpose and goals. God has always taken care of you, and isn't about to stop now. So you can seek His will without being overly concerned with your provision. **Where has worry about clothes and other necessities taken your focus away from doing God's will? Are you anxious about those things? What has this anxiety cost you in terms of joy and creativity? Are you living the life you want or feel you have to live to earn money?** *Lord, You are a good provider and have never failed my family or me. Forgive me for being worried and anxious about things beyond my control, and help me focus on Your will for my life. I commit to trust You for the basics of life so I am free to pursue Your will and work for my life.*

October 17
Jesus is Listening

"Overhearing what they said, Jesus told him, 'Don't be afraid; just believe'" - Mark 5:36.

Out of your heart your mouth speaks. What's more, Jesus is listening to what you say. It is therefore important that you align your words with your faith level or perhaps you should listen to your words to determine at what level your faith is. **As Jesus listens to your conversations, what would He say about your faith? Do you speak hopeful and expectant words of faith, or pessimistic words that show you don't expect much to happen beyond what you consider normal? Should faith maintain the ordinary or take you to the**

extraordinary? *Lord, I know You have been listening to my words and they have not been full of faith these days. Forgive me for my negativity and lack of trust. I have been afraid to speak faith for fear I would be criticized for trying to 'name it and claim it' or out of fear of being disappointed.*

October 18
Perfect Faith

"Immediately the boy's father exclaimed, 'I do believe; help me overcome my unbelief!'"
- Mark 9:24.

The father in this story wanted his son to be healed and had faith, but it wasn't perfect faith. He cried out for God to help him and Jesus granted his desire and healed his son. This is certainly good news for you. Your faith doesn't have to be perfect and doubt-free for it to be effective. You simply have to wrestle with the imperfections and not allow them to rule the day. **Do you let your doubts disturb your faith? Do your doubts keep you from moving in faith? Does the fact that you have doubts cause you to think that your faith is ruined and inoperative?** *Lord, I have faith! Today I am set free. I realize that my faith does not have to be perfect, but it has to be dominant over all other considerations. From this point I know You will help me overcome my unbelief as I stand firm on the faith I have.*

October 19
Shy Away

"Therefore I tell you, whatever you ask for in prayer, believe that you have received it, and it will be yours" - Mark 11:24.

What Jesus said here has caused no small amount of controversy, misunderstanding and misapplication. Some would probably wish He had not uttered them for this has raised the expectations of many who have not received that for which they asked. Yet Jesus did speak these words so they must be true, but wrongly applied for them not to be effective. **What is your application of these words to your prayer life? Why don't you receive more answers to prayer? What role does faith play in this transaction that Jesus described? Is this simply 'name it and claim it' or does it contain important truth for your walk with the Lord?** *Lord, I shy away from these words of Yours so that I don't misapply them or make a mistake. Yet in shying away my prayer life has been grossly anemic. Help me have a vision for my petition and see the answer so clearly I can thank You for what is to come, believing I already have it.*

October 20
The Blessing of Faith

"'Blessed is she who has believed that the Lord would fulfill his promises to her!'" - Luke 1:45.

This is what the angel Gabriel said to Mary when she responded positively and in faith to his announcement of her pregnancy. That is how God works: He promises and expects you to trust Him to fulfill the promises before you see results. Your faith response is what holds the blessing, for it enables you to see and savor the promise long before the results are evident. **Has the Lord made promises to you? What are they? Have you received them in faith? Are you living in the blessing of those promises every day, even though you don't see when or how they can come about?** *Lord, I read Your word and listen for Your voice and I hear Your promises.*

Today I understand that I am blessed when I receive them in faith, not just when I ultimately receive the end result of those promises. Thank You for Your faithfulness that allows me to live in the blessing of faith every day.

October 21
Roots

"Those on the rocky ground are the ones who receive the word with joy when they hear it, but they have no root. They believe for a while, but in the time of testing they fall away" - Luke 8:13.

It is possible to lose faith when times of testing come, not your saving faith, but faith for something or in your ability to do something. Your faith will be tested, usually requiring you to walk in the truth of your promise while circumstances and time seem to indicate that it - the fulfilled promise - will never become reality. **Are you being tested in your faith to believe God for something to happen in or with your life? Are you being true to the promise or succumbing to the circumstances? Are you putting down roots of faith, or can your faith be yanked up like a weed with shallow roots?** *Lord, I don't want to have weed faith that can be lost or easily removed in times of testing. I want to have deep roots of faith. Therefore help me focus on You and the promise and not circumstances. Help me realize I am just one phone call or meeting away from seeing the results of my faith dream.*

October 22
Controlling Fear

"Hearing this, Jesus said to Jairus, 'Don't be afraid; just believe, and she will be healed'" - Luke 8:50.

The report came that Jairus' daughter was dead. Jesus told Jairus to ignore the report and trust God, for his daughter's healing was still within reach if he controlled his fear and exercised faith. That is a good formula for you to follow: listen to Jesus and not the circumstances, control your fear and maintain your faith focus. **Where are you focusing on a negative report about the facts? Are you afraid because of what you have seen or heard? Can you see how important it is to restore and maintain your faith focus?** *Lord, I am aware that I have a tendency to focus on what is seen rather than what is unseen. Faith requires that I learn to focus on You and not on the situation in which I find myself, otherwise I succumb to fear. Teach me to keep my eyes on You and speak to me as You did to Jairus to help me when I stumble.*

October 23
Flow

"Whoever believes in me, as Scripture has said, rivers of living water will flow from within them"
- John 7:38.

When you put faith in Christ, then living water emanates from you that brings life to those around you. The water that flows from you should not be bitter or salty, but should taste like you - flavored with your gifts, purpose, experiences, perspective and unique wisdom. These waters should not be artificially flavored as you try to be someone other than who God made you to be. **Are waters flowing from you due to your faith in Christ? Are these waters flowing from you freely and with great force? Who is being touched and sustained by your waters?** *Lord, I want my faith in You to impact others and that means I must not dam up the water that*

You want to flow from me. My fear of being myself can be one thing that stops my waters, along with trying to be someone other than who You intended me to be. From this day forward I will let my inner waters flow.

October 24
The End of Faith

"Then the man said, 'Lord, I believe,' and he worshiped him" - John 9:38.

When Jesus healed and then confronted the man born blind, the man declared his faith in Christ and that faith led him to worship Jesus. That is the supreme end of faith - not to receive the object or desires of your faith but to worship the Author of your faith, that author being Jesus. Your faith is not only a commodity with which you make transactions with God, but also the source of your relationship with God. **Is your faith growing? If so, is your worship and adoration for God growing? Are you using faith to get things from God or as a means to get to God?** *Lord, I worship You for who You are, not for what You can do for me. Yet You do so much and have always rewarded my faith not only by meeting my needs but with Your presence. I take this moment to thank You and worship You as my Lord and King and I exalt You as Lord above all.*

October 25
Perpetual Doubt

"Even after Jesus had performed so many signs in their presence, they still would not believe in him" - John 12:37.

It is easy to think, "**What was wrong with those

Jews? If I had been there I would have seen what Jesus did and believed!" Yet Jesus does just as many miracles today and people still don't believe; maybe even you fit that description. If God has done great things for you in your past but you still live in fear and doubt today then you are in some ways just like Jesus' contemporaries. **Has God always provided for you but you live in constant fear of lack? Did He miraculously provide for you to do something but today you refuse to act until you see some sign of His presence? Do you live in perpetual doubt that God can do something for others but you are not sure He will and can do it for you?** *Lord, I see that I can be like those Jews I have judged and dismissed as fools for not believing. I am just as guilty for I have many testimonies of Your faithfulness to me but act today like I have none. Forgive me for my stubbornness, hardness of heart and unbelief.*

October 26
Simple Formula

---

*"Do not let your hearts be troubled.
You believe in God; believe also in me" - John 14:1.*

Your heart does not have to be troubled if you don't want it to be. Jesus told His followers to be careful *not* to allow their hearts to be in turmoil. **And what was Jesus next command?** To have faith in Him! So let's summarize. You can keep your heart free from fear, anxiety and trouble, and the way to do that is to put your faith and trust in Jesus. That seems a pretty straightforward and simple formula for inner peace. **Is your heart troubled about something? Can you see that you have control over whether or not it is? What steps can you take today to bring peace to your heart?** *Lord, I see Your formula for my peace and it* seems almost beyond my reach. My heart seems to be troubled often, but today I see it is because I allow it to be! Help me to follow Your simple formula that allows me to realize my faith is small when my heart is in turmoil.

October 27
Evidence

"Believe me when I say that I am in the Father and the Father is in me; or at least believe on the evidence of the works themselves" - John 14:11.

In this verse Jesus said that faith is within the realm of reason, saying if you can't believe based on who He is or what He says, then base your belief on what He does. When you see Jesus' works you should conclude that He is worthy of your faith. So faith is not a feeling but can be a logical decision based on God's observed goodness and grace. Take a moment today to reflect on God's goodness and then make a decision to trust Him in an area where you have allowed fear and doubt to rule your mind. **Where in your life do you have enough evidence of God's goodness that you can make a decision to trust Him regardless of how you feel?** *Lord, I choose to trust You because of the evidence of the work You have done in my life and in the lives of those around me. In light of this evidence, I put my faith in You, not just for salvation, but for the fulfillment of the promises You have made to me through Your Word.*

October 28
Reach Out

"Then he said to Thomas, 'Put your finger here; see my hands. Reach out your hand and put it into my side. Stop doubting and believe'" - John 20:27.

Jesus commanded Doubting Thomas to do what he had to do to go beyond his doubts to faith. The command indicates that it is within your capacity to decide to have faith. If you go looking for reasons to doubt you will find them. If you choose to find faith you will find that too. The choice is yours. **What can you do today to reach out and find faith? Why is it so easy for you to focus on the doubts? Do you know that Jesus commands you, just like He did Thomas, to stop doubting and believe?** *Lord, I confess that I am like Thomas, finding all kinds of reasons to talk myself out of faith into doubt. I have made the excuse that I'm only human and that faith is too difficult or only for a chosen few special people. Today I vow to reach out and touch something that will enhance and feed my faith!*

October 29
Hearing From God

"'If you are the Messiah,' they said, 'tell us.' Jesus answered, 'If I tell you, you will not believe me'"
- Luke 22:67.

You may say, "I need to hear from the Lord and then I will have faith. So I will wait on Him to initiate and focus my faith." In today's verse Jesus said that when He speaks, it is no guarantee that anyone will have faith. This means if you are not careful you can read His word or hear His voice and not believe what Jesus is saying! **Have you refused to have faith in any area of your life that the Lord has been addressing? Have your assumptions about God, who He is or what He will do affected your ability to hear and have faith? Do you have the courage to ask God to show you where those areas in your life are?** *Lord, I ask You today to show me where I am not believing what You said,* *whether in Your word or in Your other communication to me. In advance, I ask Your forgiveness and I commit today to walk in faith by believing what it is that You say, no matter what my bias or preconceived notions may be.*

October 30
Non-Sensical

"But they did not believe the women, because their words seemed to them like nonsense" - Luke 24:11.

People can give you a good faith report that has the potential to stimulate and massage your faith, but if you don't listen carefully you can dismiss their words as non-sensical. When their report doesn't match your picture of reality you can miss your opportunity to grow your faith. Your mind picture of what God can do for *you* needs to change or you will dismiss their testimony and remain in your unbelief. **Where is your mindset set for non-faith? Whose testimony have you dismissed instead of welcomed? Where are you missing faith because you consider it non-sensical - not making sense?** *Lord, You are faithful and have sent many messengers to awaken my faith, but I have sometimes refused their report. The problem is my thinking, which made their words sound like nonsense, when in reality I am the non-sensical one. Deliver me Lord from my faith-destructive need to be so sensible!*

October 31
Blind Spots

"He said to them, 'How foolish you are, and how slow to believe all that the prophets have spoken! Did not the Messiah have to suffer these things and then enter his glory?'" - Luke 24:25-26.

The disciples on the Emmaus Road could not recognize Jesus even though they were well acquainted with Him because they thought He was dead. Your thinking determines what you hear and see, even where God is concerned. These disciples were slow to believe and that made them foolish in Jesus' estimation. **Where are you slow to believe what the prophets have written? Where are you reading Scripture but not comprehending because of your thinking? What is God trying to show you that you are blocking because of your mindset and perspective?** *Lord I am foolish, just like those disciples on the road. I am walking with You, but I don't always hear or recognize You because of my small and limited thinking. Deliver me from these blind spots that prevent me from entering by faith into all You have for me where my purpose and goals are concerned.*

November

Gold Mine Principle 1

Purpose

November 1
Seeking You

"Joseph had a dream, and when he told it to his brothers, they hated him all the more"
- Genesis 37:5.

Joseph did not go looking for purpose; his purpose came looking for him. One night when his conscious defenses were down, God sent him a dream that he would be the leader of all his brothers and family, even though he was not the oldest. In fact, God sent him two dreams just to confirm His choice and Joseph's purpose. **What situation or problem always seems to seek and find you? What has the Lord shown you about you that He has not shown anyone else? What calling or purpose sets you apart from everyone else?** *Lord, I have often made purpose my personal quest when it is not a quest at all - it is a response to Your initiative and call in my life. Today I rest in Your ability to communicate with me and not my ability to seek or hear. I accept my distinctive purpose before I know what it is and I thank You for it.*

November 2
Opposition

"His brothers said to him, 'Do you intend to reign over us? Will you actually rule us?' And they hated him all the more because of his dream and what he had said" - Genesis 37:8.

Characters in the Bible often did not have an enemy until they began to pursue purpose. David, Solomon, Saul of Tarsus and even Jesus attracted opposition when they began their purpose quest. This means there are two things you need to remember. First, not everyone will celebrate or cooperate with your purpose, for it can be a threat to them in some fashion. Second, your enemies don't indicate you are doing something wrong but something right where purpose is concerned. **Do you have enemies who oppose who you are and what you do?** If not, then perhaps you are not focused enough on purpose. **If so, are you fretting because everyone doesn't like you and is that keeping you from fulfilling your purpose to the fullest?** *Lord, I admit that at times I seek the favor of men in such a way that it hinders me from serving You to the fullest. I ask You to set me free from the opinions of others, but not so much that I can't hear Your voice of adjustment through them. Help me not to allow them to intimidate me away from purpose.*

November 3
Others

***"When he told his father as well as his brothers, his father rebuked him and said, 'What is this dream you had? Will your mother and I and your brothers actually come and bow down to the ground before you?' His brothers were jealous of him, but his father kept the matter in mind"* - Genesis 37:10-11.**

It is interesting that when Joseph shared his dreams his family knew exactly what they meant. They recognized that he was going to rule over them, but in their state of mind they could not see how that could ever be. Otherscan often discern and recognize your purpose and will confirm it if you don't dismiss what they say as irrelevant. **What have you heard from others that could be God's purpose message to you? Are you dismissing what they say, stubbornly clinging to**

your own limited perspective? *Lord, I acknowledge that I can be stiff-necked, refusing to hear or receive anything that does not align with my own self-image of who I believe myself to be. Help me to be more pliable and receptive to consider other viewpoints of my purpose and capabilities.*

November 4
Jesus, A Man of Purpose

"For the Son of Man came to seek and to save the lost" - Luke 19:10.

Jesus had a purpose. It enabled Him to say no to the Pharisees who wanted to spend time with Him. What's more, Jesus never had to go looking for the lost; the lost always came looking for Him. Jesus also had seemingly chance encounters with the lost that were actually examples of Him fulfilling His purpose, like this story of Zacchaeus in Luke 19. **What or who is it that always seems to find you? What chance encounters have a consistent theme that can help you identify your purpose? Do you know your purpose well enough that you can say 'no' to non-purposeful opportunities?** *Lord, I want to know my purpose so well that I can recognize it when it seeks me out; so well, that I can seek out opportunities to fulfill it with confidence and skill. In other words, I want to be a person of purpose like Jesus! Help me to be this kind of purposeful person today and every day for the rest of my life.*

November 5
Restoration

"The one who does what is sinful is of the devil, because the devil has been sinning from the

beginning. The reason the Son of God appeared was to destroy the devil's work" - 1 John 3:8.

The devil tempted Adam and Eve who fell into sin. That sin did not just impact their relationship with the Lord, but also marred their purpose (rule over God's creation), their creativity (Adam had just named the animals) and their ability to work as a team. In today's verse John told us that Jesus came to destroy the devil's work. In other words, Jesus came to restore purpose, creativity and teamwork, in addition to man's relationship with God. **Are you asking Jesus for help to find and fulfill your purpose? Are you immersed in God-given creativity? Is your ability to work with others improving?** *Lord, I see that Jesus' work on the cross is so much more than for forgiveness of my sin, as important as that is. He came to restore what the devil had stolen and part of that is my purpose! I ask You to give me a fresh understanding of who I am in You and then to release me afresh to do it in Your name.*

November 6
A Servant's Heart

"Just as the Son of Man did not come to be served, but to serve, and to give his life as a ransom for many" - Matthew 20:28.

Your purpose positions you to serve with excellence and skill. You won't simply be a polite person (like opening doors for others, which is not really service) but will use the power of your expertise and anointing to equip others for success and meet their needs. If Jesus came to serve in the power of His purpose, then you can be sure that you are called to do the same thing. **Are you using your purpose and goals to serve others'**

needs or your own? Do you see purpose mainly as a source of self-expression or as a means to serve with distinction and effectiveness? *Lord, I know that Jesus came to serve, but not just to do anything, rather to seek and save the lost. He served with purpose and function in His purpose. It is my goal to do the same things. Give me a servant's heart, help me see the world's needs through the eyes of my purpose and then to give my life to meet those needs.*

November 7
Let Them Shine

"Mordecai had a cousin named Hadassah, whom he had brought up because she had neither father nor mother. This young woman, who was also known as Esther, had a lovely figure and was beautiful. Mordecai had taken her as his own daughter when her father and mother died" - Esther 2:7.

Esther was an orphan but she grew up to be a woman with a lovely figure and beautiful face. Those attributes were from the Lord and God used them for His purpose and glory. You also have attributes and characteristics for which you had nothing to do (so you should not be proud), but which God wants to use if you will allow them to be seen and heard. You could also call those things your strengths. **What are those attributes, do you know? Have you built your life and ministry around those strengths? What more can you do to allow them to shine for God's glory?** *Lord, I accept the fact that You have put things in me for which You expect a return on Your investment. It is inconsistent that You would give me light and then want me to hide it. I commit to exhibit my strengths, whatever they are, for You to direct and use as You see fit.*

November 8
Beauty

"She pleased him and won his favor. Immediately he provided her with her beauty treatments and special food" - Esther 3:9.

Esther won the beauty contest by winning the king's favor. The king entrusted her to his aide who was assigned an interesting task: his job was to make Esther even more beautiful! There is a lesson here for you: God gave you gifts and strengths and wants you to work and make them more effective and stronger. **Do you know what your strengths are? Are you embracing or belittling them? What are you doing to make your 'beauty' even more spectacular?** *Lord, I don't want to hide my beauty, whether it is in music, art, business or speech. First, I accept the fact You gave me my strengths and I have a responsibility to acknowledge and honor them. Then I commit to develop my beauty by taking lessons, reading or doing anything necessary to make them sparkle.*

November 9
God Will Not Wait

"For if you remain silent at this time, relief and deliverance for the Jews will arise from another place, but you and your father's family will perish. And who knows but that you have come to your royal position for such a time as this?" - Esther 4:14.

At times you must wait to fulfill your purpose until the right time in history comes for it to occur. Many do not want to get ahead of the Lord, however, so they risk forfeiting their opportunity to make an impact when the season comes and the door opens. God will not wait but He will raise up others to fulfill your purpose if you are hesitant or fearful. **Are you getting ready for your purpose opportunity? Are you passive or aggressive where purpose is concerned? Do you see that waiting on the Lord is fine but when He moves the waiting is over?** *Lord, I want and need the proper mindset where purpose is concerned. I cannot have an attitude that it will all work out with or without me when You have given me something to do. That means I must prepare to move; when You open the door I must walk through it with confidence. Help me, Lord, to be ready!*

November 10
A Promise

"Blessed is she who has believed that the Lord would fulfill his promises to her!" - Luke 1:45.

When you discover your purpose you often have no idea how to fulfill it. In some sense your purpose is a promise that God makes and then you have faith that He will work out the details and process. You simply accept your purpose and relax, but then respond to God's initiatives as He opens doors for you to develop yourself and express your purpose - just like Mary did. **Has God made the promise of purpose to you? Are you fretting over how your purpose is going to work out? Do you need to release the details to Him, relax and rejoice in the fact that God knows your name and has assigned you purposeful work?** *Lord, I have never seen purpose as Your promise to me but today I do! It's a promise of who I will be and what I will do, but You express it in the 'now' as if it already exists. That's where my faith comes in to play. I trust You, Lord, as the Author and Finisher of my purpose.*

November 11
Praise

"Praise be to the name of God for ever and ever; wisdom and power are his. He changes times and seasons; he deposes kings and raises up others. He gives wisdom to the wise and knowledge to the discerning. He reveals deep and hidden things; he knows what lies in darkness, and light dwells with him" - Daniel 2:20b-22.

These are the words of Daniel when he took on the seemingly impossible task of interpreting the king's dream when the king refused to tell him the dream! The wise men were sentenced to die, but Daniel stood in the gap and sought the Lord for the interpretation, which God gave him. In some sense Daniel's praise reveals his purpose - to reveal deep and hidden things that lurk in the dark, which he did again and again. **What do you volunteer to do that others shy away from? What excites you so much that you praise God for your involvement and its fulfillment?** *Lord, there are some things that intimidate others but not me, and that may very well hold clues to my purpose. When I get results in those areas I praise You, which is another indication of my purpose. Help me see what those things are so I can unlock the mystery of my purpose as Daniel did his.*

November 12
Stubborn Heart

"When the angel of the Lord appeared to Gideon, he said, 'The Lord is with you, mighty warrior'" - Judges 6:12.

Gideon was acting like anything but mighty when the

angel appeared to him. What's more, Gideon objected and even scoffed at the Lord's descriptive label. When you first see your purpose you can also be dismissive, thinking you are too young, too old, too uneducated, too frail or weak. Yet the Lord sees you as you will be, not as you are, because He is confident His grace is sufficient to get the job done. **Are you like Gideon, thinking there is no way you can be a person of purpose? Are you dismissing God's will for your life as impossible or improbable? Are you walking in your own or God's perspective of your capabilities?** *Lord, I need to change my thinking regarding purpose. Purpose is Your will for my life, which means You will empower me regardless of how I feel. Forgive me for my stubborn heart that refuses to accept Your testimony of me; help me walk in the power of Your purpose presence.*

November 13
More Deeply

"When I heard these things, I sat down and wept. For some days I mourned and fasted and prayed before the God of heaven" - Nehemiah 1:4.

One has to assume that many people heard the report about the disrepair in Jerusalem, but it affected Nehemiah more than others. **Why is that?** Because Nehemiah's purpose was to rebuild Jerusalem, so the news would obviously impact him more severely. The same is true for your purpose. News, a cause or a dilemma may touch many, but it will touch you more deeply if it is connected to your purpose. **What makes you cry? What moves you and you cannot understand why it doesn't impact others the way it does you? What causes you to intercede with God about the situation?** Your answers are an indication of where your purpose lies. *Lord, I have often wondered why I am more affected by certain things than others and today I realize it's because those 'things' are somehow tied to my purpose. Help me see the connection and then help me not to complain about others' insensitivity but rather to accept this as my duty to act on what I see.*

November 14
The Key

"Nehemiah said, 'Go and enjoy choice food and sweet drinks, and send some to those who have nothing prepared. This day is holy to our Lord. Do not grieve, for the joy of the Lord is your strength'" - Nehemiah 8:10.

This verse holds the most important key to finding, sustaining and fulfilling purpose - joy. God creates you with joy to do certain things so you will gravitate toward them - thus you will know and have an incentive to do His will. When you deny that joy is important and replace it with responsibility or duty, you lose your joy and consequently your strength. **Do you experience joy in what you do? How often do you do it? Are you out of strength because you are cut off from or denying your joy?** *Lord, I have been taught not to trust joy, thinking it may be frivolous or childish. Yet You created me to have and experience it and I have cut myself off from joy due to bad thinking. I embrace my joy today and agree to do what it leads me to do as often as possible.*

November 15
Service

"Each day one ox, six choice sheep and some poultry were prepared for me, and every ten days

an abundant supply of wine of all kinds. In spite of all this, I never demanded the food allotted to the governor, because the demands were heavy on these people" - Nehemiah 5:18.

Nehemiah's purpose was to rebuild Jerusalem, but it was not a source of personal gain. Nehemiah's purpose led him to a life of service, something God had instilled in him as a butler in Persia serving a pagan king. Your purpose is usually assigned to alleviate the pain or enhance the lives of others, and you become their servant, serving them in God's power. **Where do you serve with the greatest effectiveness and joy? Can that area be related to your purpose? Are you enriching others or yourself in your pursuit of purposeful work?** *Lord, I accept Your call to a life of service, but I want it to be effective service based on Your power expressed through my purpose. Deliver me from a limited view of service so I can make an impact in my world according to Your purposeful will for my life.*

November 16
Legacy

"Remember me for this, my God, and do not blot out what I have so faithfully done for the house of my God and its services . . . Remember me for this also, my God, and show mercy to me according to your great love" - Nehemiah 13:14, 22.

Nehemiah's prayer included an appeal to be remembered for what he had done and not for who he was or what he had not done - sins he had not committed. The point is that your purpose will provide a legacy for you and will enable you to talk to God as Nehemiah did: with intimacy and conviction. **Are you** building a legacy of what you are doing or out of what you are not doing? Can you boldly pray like Nehemiah, asking God to remember you?** *Lord, Nehemiah's prayers were bold and I want to pray like that as well. I also want you to remember me for what I have done for You as I express and fulfill my purpose.*

November 17
Purpose Points

"So Samuel took the horn of oil and anointed him in the presence of his brothers, and from that day on the Spirit of the Lord came powerfully upon David" - 1 Samuel 16:13.

There are several purpose points in this verse. First, David was anointed in front of his brothers. Your purpose is always a public event, for it is often meant to be carried out for others in full view. Then this anointing indicated David had power from God to do what he was created to do. Finally, the anointing meant David would achieve specific results. **What are you anointed to do? Are you bashful or hesitant to carry out your purpose in public because of attention it will draw? Are you bearing fruit and results that glorify God and serve people?** *Lord, I want Your Spirit's presence in my life, which means I will produce results in a certain area of endeavor. I acknowledge I cannot do what You have assigned me without Your anointing. What's more, I accept the fact that my purpose will draw attention to me as I carry it out before people who need what I do.*

November 18
Inadequacy

"'Woe to me!' I cried. 'I am ruined!

> *For I am a man of unclean lips, and*
> *I live among a people of unclean lips,*
> *and my eyes have seen the King,*
> *the Lord Almighty'" - Isaiah 6:5.*

Your purpose almost always dredges up a sense of your own unworthiness and inability to carry out what the Lord assigns. And in the natural it's true - you cannot accomplish what you see your purpose to be without God's help. Yet the Lord knows your limitations when He chooses you and the good news is that He goes with you as you seek to carry out His will. **Are you battling a sense of unworthiness or ineffectiveness where purpose is concerned? Are you allowing fear to use that sense to keep you from preparing for or trying to fulfill your purpose?** *Lord, I am unworthy to have You call or use me, yet in Your grace You use all of us already knowing our inadequacies. It is an expression of your grace that You want to use me, so I accept Your grace in the midst of my personal awareness of my sin and shortcomings. Help me move past me to You and Your purpose.*

November 19
Volunteering

> *"Then I heard the voice of the Lord saying, 'Whom shall I send? And who will go for us?' And I said, 'Here am I. Send me!'" - Isaiah 6:8.*

While Isaiah confronted his own inadequacy it did not stop him from enthusiastically volunteering to go and do God's will. There are some who see this as 'self-promoting,' thinking that Isaiah should have waited and allowed God to make His choice. Yet it is commendable that he offered himself quickly and freely to do God's will, and God took him up on the offer. **Are you holding back, concerned that you are promoting yourself instead of aggressively moving forward in your purpose? Are you letting the Lord know that you are ready now to do His will? Are you listening for God's invitation to go and do?** *Lord, I see Isaiah's willingness to go and do Your will, and I am challenged - challenged to be as forthright as he was, challenged to listen more carefully for Your call, challenged to respond quickly and eagerly to do Your will. Deliver me from wrong thinking where self-promotion is concerned so I can respond to You.*

November 20
Service Prep

"But Jehoshaphat asked, 'Is there no prophet of the Lord here, through whom we may inquire of the Lord?' An officer of the king of Israel answered, 'Elisha son of Shaphat is here. He used to pour water on the hands of Elijah'" - 2 Kings 3:11.

It is interesting that the king's official knew Elisha because of his service to Elijah - note that he poured water on Elijah's hands. His service to Elijah was personal and practical. It prepared Elisha for his own purpose and ministry and gained him a reputation among all the tribes of Israel. **In what ways do you serve? Do you see service as preparation for purpose? How can you employ a service strategy to help advance your purpose?** *Lord, I want to be known as a servant. There is only one way for that to happen and that is to serve and do it with distinction. Open my eyes to the service possibilities around me and then allow me to serve with excellence, trusting You to open* *purpose doors for me as I show my servant's heart to You and others.*

November 21
Hang in There

"Elisha then picked up Elijah's cloak that had fallen from him and went back and stood on the bank of the Jordan" - 2 Kings 2:13.

Elisha was present when Elijah, his mentor, was taken up into heaven. Elisha picked up his mentor's coat and parted the waters of the Jordan River, proving that God was with him as He had been with Elijah. The point is that Elisha hung in until the end and was rewarded with his own purposeful ministry. You need to endure as well no matter how long it takes to reach your vision or goal. **Are you tired of waiting and serving? Does it seem like the promise of God will never arrive where you are concerned? To whom do you need to stay close until your purpose is fulfilled?** *Lord, I want to be a servant, but I want it to be faithful and hang in there so that you can promote me in due time. Help me be present spiritually and mentally when the time of my promotion arrives and allow me to learn from my mentors all I need to learn to do Your will.*

November 22
Creative Prayer

"So give your servant a discerning heart to govern your people and to distinguish between right and wrong. For who is able to govern this great people of yours?" - 1 Kings 3:9.

Solomon's purpose was to govern with wisdom and that

purpose affected and directed his prayer life. In today's verse he made his famous request for a discerning or listening heart and God was pleased to grant his request. Your prayer life reflects what it God has created you to do, so that begs the questions: **What or whom do you pray for regularly? Can you see patterns in your prayer requests that can help identify your purpose? Are you maximizing your prayer time with specific creative requests or is your prayer list rather staid and boring?** *Lord, help me reinvigorate my prayer life by making bold and practical requests that enhance my ability to find and fulfill my purpose. I need You every step of the way, along with Your wisdom and creativity. Open my eyes to the power of prayer that is more than just petition, but vibrant two-way communication.*

November 23
Your Role

"The Lord was pleased that Solomon had asked for this. So God said to him, 'Since you have asked for this and not for long life or wealth for yourself, nor have asked for the death of your enemies but for discernment in administering justice, I will do what you have asked. I will give you a wise and discerning heart, so that there will never have been anyone like you, nor will there ever be'" - 1 Kings 3:10-12.

God distinguished Solomon from all other kings because of Solomon's prayer, which pleased the Lord immensely. This prayer was a function of Solomon's freewill. Solomon had many options of what to pray, but he chose wisely and God was moved to make him a great king. **What is in your heart to pray and ask? Are you praying boldly and creatively where your purpose and goals are concerned? Are you putting** off for God to do what only you can do? *Lord, I need to take responsibility for my prayers where purpose is concerned. I have been afraid to ask You for too much out of fear that I am doing something wrong. I need to have faith, which pleases You. Help me understand my role so I am not waiting for You to do what only I can do.*

November 24
Heart Prep

"Joshua son of Nun, who had been Moses' aide since youth, spoke up and said, 'Moses, my lord, stop them!'" - Numbers 11:28.

Like Elisha, Joshua's preparation for purpose was to serve someone else. This gave him valuable insight into how Moses thought and acted, but it probably also dealt with Joshua's pride and ambition in preparation for him to be the leader. God empowers you for purpose, but you cannot ignore the heart prep required to ensure that you will stay grounded as you enjoy purpose success. **How is your attitude these days – arrogant, or humble and pliable? Are you serving others to get close and learn? Are you preparing your heart today for purpose success tomorrow?** *Lord, I need to pay attention to my attitude and heart condition as I pursue excellence expressing my purpose. Join me to others whom I can serve so that I can learn and be more conformed to Christ's image. I don't want my character to undermine my effectiveness, but I need Your help to prep my heart.*

November 25
Spirit of Purpose

"So the Lord said to Moses, 'Take Joshua son of

Nun, a man in whom is the spirit of leadership, and lay your hand on him'" - Numbers 27:18.

According to this verse and translation, Joshua had the spirit of leadership. Other versions just say 'Spirit.' The Spirit of God was present in Joshua's life to make him a leader and the Spirit is with and in you to help you fulfill your purpose as well. Therefore you have the Spirit of crafts, or the Spirit of acting, or the Spirit of business, or the Spirit of children's ministry in you. **Can you identify what version of the Spirit you have in you? Do you see that you will operate in divine efficiency and results when you flow in your purpose? Where are you under-living the power of purpose that resides in you?** *Lord, I know the Spirit resides in me, but I never saw before today that He resides to do something not just in me but through me. I see now that I flow in the power of the Spirit whenever I function in purpose. I have been under-living my potential, but no more. From now on I will truly operate in the Spirit.*

November 26
Youth

"You will become pregnant and have a son whose head is never to be touched by a razor because the boy is to be a Nazirite, dedicated to God from the womb. He will take the lead in delivering Israel from the hands of the Philistines" - Judges 13:5.

Samson's mother knew his purpose before he was born. She was told how to shape him to be a Nazirite so that his strength would be in his relationship and connection with the Lord. (Nazirites had a restricted diet and did not cut their hair.) If you are a parent, aunt, uncle or even a close friend, you can help shape and nurture purpose in someone else because God wants them to know and prepare. The best thing you can do is help focus and direct their relationship with the Lord. **Are you involved in the life or lives of young people, even if you are young yourself? What are you doing to help instill a sense of purpose rather than career in these youth? What more can you do?** *Lord, You are a God of purpose not just for me, but also for others. And you often reveal purpose at an early age, sometimes even before children are born. I make myself available as a purpose coach and trainer to help youth around me in my church, family or school to be people of purpose according to Your will.*

November 27
Revelation

"'Come, follow me,' Jesus said, 'and I will send you out to fish for people'" - *Matthew 4:19.*

Jesus identified the purpose for Peter and Andrew when He first met them. There is no special timing as to when God reveals your purpose, but often it is when you are ready to hear or need to know so you can spend a time preparing! What's more, your purpose is not something you figure out or go to a seminar to learn how to identify. It is a revelation to you from the Lord! **What has the Lord showed you about you? Are you asking and listening? Are you getting ready to fulfill it if you already know it?** *Lord, I want to know my purpose and I need You to show me what it is! Help me to see it, then help me express it. All the while I want to follow You and not just pursue purpose, for without You, my purpose is empty and humanistic. You are my purpose focus; speak, Lord!*

November 28
Hair

"And she made a vow, saying, 'Lord Almighty, if you will only look on your servant's misery and remember me, and not forget your servant but give her a son, then I will give him to the Lord for all the days of his life, and no razor will ever be used on his head'" - 1 Samuel 1:11.

In this verse, Hannah, the mother of Samuel, identified her unborn son's purpose and dedicated him to the Lord as a Nazirite just like Samson's mother did. The Nazirites did not cut their hair, symbolic of the rule that whatever came from 'within' a Nazirite was not to be touched by human hands - it belonged to the Lord and was to be shaped and fashioned by Him alone. Parents are to cooperate with God's plan for their children and not shape it according to what they think is best; children are to recognize what God has done in them and submit and cooperate fully. **Are you allowing your 'hair' to grow and take the shape that God has chosen? Are you allowing the same to happen for the loved ones in your world?** *Lord, I want my spiritual 'hair' to be just as You intended, without me fooling with its shape, color or length. It is Yours to do with what You want. The hair of my family and friends is also your business, and I refuse to put my hands on it according to what I think is best. May Your purpose reign supreme in our lives!*

November 29
Your Purpose Land

"Go, walk through the length and breadth of the land, for I am giving it to you" - Genesis 13:17.

No matter how far you are in understanding your purpose, there is still a faith aspect to it. Once you receive your purpose it is like the land promised to Abraham - you have a ways to go until you possess it. That should not stop you from 'walking' your purpose land to enjoy what it will be when you have eventually become an author, actor, business owner, or world traveler. **Are you walking your purpose land today? Have you discovered its outer boundaries? Are you visualizing what it will be and in some sense already is?** *Lord, I am a child of Abraham, which means I walk by faith. Both finding and fulfilling purpose are faith ventures, but that doesn't mean I cannot savor my purpose now, even though it's in the beginning or unseen stages. Help me see more clearly so I can walk my purpose land today!*

November 30
Family Ties

"'Don't be afraid,' he said. 'My father Saul will not lay a hand on you. You will be king over Israel, and I will be second to you. Even my father Saul knows this'" - 1 Samuel 23:17.

David reached his purpose but Jonathan did not. Even though Jonathan knew his purpose, he could never break away from his family expectations and the manipulations of his father, Saul, and it cost him not only his purpose but also his life. Be careful the same doesn't happen to you. You are to love and honor your family, but your purpose is between you and the Lord and no one has the right to interfere with that, no matter how close you are or how much you love them. **Is your family a hindrance in your quest for purpose? What**

are you prepared to do to change that scenario? What is it in you that God is addressing over this situation? *Lord, I love my family, but I realize that my purpose is Your will for my life, which is the highest priority. Forgive me where I have put relationships ahead of You. I ask Your grace for courage to move forward, even if that means moving away from my family ties and control as I seek to do Your will.*

December

A Potpourri of Principles

December 1
Choice

"But the Pharisees and the experts in the law rejected God's purpose for themselves, because they had not been baptized by John" - Luke 7:30.

You have a choice in purpose. You can choose never to search and find it or you can find it and for whatever reason reject it. At that point, the sovereign God will choose someone else to fulfill the plans He had for you. That doesn't mean He does not love you, but the loss is all yours as you forfeit the joys and exhilaration of being used by God for something special. **What is your attitude toward your purpose? Are you excited or indifferent? Passive or aggressive? Are you waiting or wading into the opportunity?** *Lord, I don't want to miss my purposeful life through waiting, fear or apathy. I choose to accept Your purpose assignment and I vow to pursue it with all my heart and strength out of devotion to You. I further commit to prepare myself and seize every opportunity to make a difference for Your glory! Amen.*

December 2
Your Mark

"Then Simon Peter came along behind him and went straight into the tomb. He saw the strips of linen lying there, as well as the cloth that had been wrapped around Jesus' head. The cloth was still lying in its place, separate from the linen" - John 20:6-7.

There was something about the placement of Jesus' facecloth that caught Peter's attention. It was not discarded casually or thrown on the floor of the tomb. It was lying 'in its place.' This was perhaps a distinguishing mark that belonged to Jesus, something those close to Him would have known about His attention to detail or His tendency to organize a certain way. **What is your organizing 'mark?' Is it sloppiness and haphazard work habits or is there a pattern and rhythm to your work world that is distinctive to you? What can you do to improve in this area of life?** *Lord, You built organization into Your creation, for the sun rises and sets at a predictable time, with seasons starting and ending on a certain day. I want and need that kind of structure and routine if I am going to succeed in the work You gave me to do. Help me overcome my bad habits so I can organize!*

December 3
Your Time

"'You go to the festival. I am not going up to this festival, because my time has not yet fully come.' After he had said this, he stayed in Galilee" - John 7:8-9.

The Jews had a rhythm to their year that revolved around three special festivals or holy days. This particular festival was not one of them, so Jesus initially chose not to attend. When He did go, He went on His own terms and for His own reasons. You must learn to do the same, resisting cultural, family and even church traditions to maximize the use of your time. This requires a bit of self, for you must sometimes do what's in your best interests, or at least the best interests of your purpose and high priority goals. **Are you managing your own time or is something or someone else doing it for you? Is this allowing you to fulfill your purpose and achieve your goals?** *Lord, I encounter* *a lot of expectations of how I will use my time. I need courage to resist those that are not in the best interests of my work and purpose You have assigned me. Help me step back to evaluate how I use my time and give me a plan on how to use it efficiently.*

December 4
An Email From Heaven

"Elisha then left his oxen and ran after Elijah. 'Let me kiss my father and mother goodbye,' he said, 'and then I will come with you'" - 1 Kings 19:20.

On their first encounter, Elisha went home to bid farewell to his family and followed Elijah until his death. That required tremendous faith that it wasn't just Elijah talking to Elisha, but that the Lord was speaking through him. You won't find or fulfill purpose without the same kind of faith, for you won't receive an email from heaven outlining your purpose assignment. You will have to trust that God is speaking to you through others or circumstances and then act accordingly. **Are you waiting for that email from heaven? Are you trying to move with such certainty that faith is not required? Are you trusting that you can know God's will through faith?** *Lord, I admit that I read how Elisha reacted with such certain faith and it scares me, thinking that I may have to do the same. He walked away from his world based on Elijah's world and went in a different direction. Help me to have that kind of resolve and faith, putting my trust in You completely.*

December 5
Potential

"I am a Jew, born in Tarsus of Cilicia,

but brought up in this city. I studied under Gamaliel and was thoroughly trained in the law of our ancestors. I was just as zealous for God as any of you are today" - Acts 22:3.

When Paul thought he knew his purpose as a Jew, he pursued it will great zeal and found the best mentor and training he could find. This all came in handy later when his purpose was adjusted to be an apostle. In other words, God cannot promote potential. He can only promote those who have developed their potential to the fullest. Training and education are a big part of that. **What are you doing to develop your purpose or what you think is your purpose? Are you seeking training and education as part of that development? Is reading a part of that development plan?** *Lord, I want to be the fullest, best expression of who you created me to be. Therefore, I need and want the training, knowledge and skill that will make that happen. Send me opportunities and people to develop my potential and I commit to do the work to become 'world-class' in my purpose expression.*

December 6
Bold Goal

"This day the Lord will deliver you into my hands, and I'll strike you down and cut off your head. This very day I will give the carcasses of the Philistine army to the birds and the wild animals, and the whole world will know that there is a God in Israel" - 1 Samuel 17:46.

You would have to admit that David was specific when he described his goal when confronting Goliath. He acknowledged God's help and then painted a specific picture of what he was going to do, and the eventual outcome was exactly what he described. **How clear are your goals? What is preventing you from having that kind of confidence that leads to a clear description and speech?** *Lord, I love this story, but I am not anxious to replicate it in my own life. David put himself on the line with such a bold proclamation and I am afraid to do that. What if I fail? What if I say the wrong thing? Help me, Lord, to deal with my fears and then boldly proclaim what I believe You will help me accomplish.*

December 7
Reality

"Reaching into his bag and taking out a stone, he slung it and struck the Philistine on the forehead. The stone sank into his forehead, and he fell facedown on the ground" - 1 Samuel 17:49.

David had foreseen the event described in this verse and it played out just as he had said. Yet this goal's end was not just a random act, but made possible in part by David's skill with the slingshot. The point is that goals are not just wishful thinking, but based on the reality of who you are and what God has gifted you to do. **What goals have you set that are based on the skills you have? Are you setting goals to do new things with the experience you have gathered? What big goal do you need to set and verbalize but are afraid to do so?** *Lord, I love the account of David and Goliath but I am hesitant to act like David, mostly out of fear. Yet You have given me skills and gifts and I have some wonderful testimonies of what You have done in my life. Help me to set some goals that will allow me to use all those things for You!*

December 8
Time Investment

"But Ruth replied, 'Don't urge me to leave you or to turn back from you. Where you go I will go, and where you stay I will stay. Your people will be my people and your God my God'" - Ruth 1:16.

Ruth made a decision about where she would spend her life and consequently her time based on a relationship with her mother-in-law after Ruth's husband died. That decision came from her personal values system of loyalty and love for Naomi. Both women ended up in Bethlehem where Ruth eventually met her new husband Boaz and they became the grandparents of King David. **Are your values determining where you are investing your life and time? Are you wasting time doing things you know are not connected to what's most important to you? Why is that happening in your life and what are you willing to do to change it?** *Lord, there are many other things making my time management decisions and I feel like my life is out of control. I need to be true to who I am, just like Ruth was, and trust You for the results. As the year ends I vow to look at where I am wasting my life and make some significant changes for the New Year.*

December 9
Jobs and Purpose

"The words of Amos, one of the shepherds of Tekoa—the vision he saw concerning Israel two years before the earthquake, when Uzziah was king of Judah and Jeroboam son of Jehoash was king of Israel" - Amos 1:1.

The word of the Lord came to Amos while he was a shepherd. His purpose was not to tend sheep - that was his occupation. His purpose was to hear and deliver God's word to a rebellious people. Your occupation may or may not be your career; only you determine that. It is not unusual, however, to make your money doing one thing, but to fulfill your purpose in off-work hours, just like the tentmaker Paul. **Are you currently purposely fulfilled in your career? Do you express purpose in or out of your normal workday experience? Are you looking for purpose in your career when it's simply not there?** *Lord, I thank You for the provision You give through my job, but I realize that is limiting me where purpose is concerned. Help me see clearly how I can use my off and down time to pursue and fulfill purpose while I remain faithful and committed on my job. Show me how I can do both career and purpose.*

December 10
A Trip

"Jesus and his disciples went on to the villages around Caesarea Philippi. On the way he asked them, 'Who do people say I am?'" - Mark 8:27.

When God wants to speak to you He often takes you on a trip. When you are out of your usual daily routine, you are more open to the things around you and to the Lord. This is what was happening in this verse. Jesus took the disciples far away from the hustle and bustle of Galilee and Jerusalem to a remote area to talk to them about who He was and His future suffering. It was on this trip that Peter found his purpose and the disciples discovered Jesus in a whole new way! **Is it time that you take a few days and go off with the Lord? What will you talk to Him about when you go?**

What questions will you ask? *Lord, I need some time with You, just You and me, talking about Your will and purpose for my life. I pray You would open up some time in my schedule that I can seize to make that happen. When I arrive for our appointment I am open to whatever You choose to say to and show me.*

December 11
The Pattern

"Make this tabernacle and all its furnishings exactly like the pattern I will show you"
- Exodus 25:9.

God is an excellent administrator and organizer. He knows the end from the beginning and is always on budget and on time. What's more, He is willing to share His 'expertise' with any and all who ask. Therefore you would be wise to call on Him to organize your world, whatever that involves, whether family, ministry or business, into wherever your purpose may take you. **Do you need organizational help? Can you humble yourself and admit that you need that help? How can you draw on God's wisdom - through others, His Word or the example of historical figures?** *Lord, I don't want my world to run itself because I have shrunk it to its most manageable size. I want to do and have all You intend for me and no matter how large to me, it's all manageable to You. Give me wisdom for how to organize my world and I vow to apply what You show me, according to the pattern You reveal.*

December 12
Heart Attack

"See to it, brothers and sisters, that none

of you has a sinful, unbelieving heart that turns away from the living God" - Hebrews 3:12.

You are to 'see to it' that you don't have an unbelieving heart. That indicates that a faith-less heart is your decision and under your control. When you don't take care of your heart and faith, then you turn away from God, and that is fatal where purpose and goals go. This makes perfect sense, for without faith it is impossible to please God. **Is your heart full of faith? Do you see un-faith as being a sin or simply a weakness? Do you accept the responsibility of keeping your heart in a good faith condition?** *Lord, I don't want to have a heart attack of unbelief. Therefore I choose to trust You, not just for salvation, but also for all the affairs of life, including purpose and goals. Help me keep watch over my heart and to know when it is weak in faith, so I can correct that condition immediately by Your grace.*

December 13
God Has a Plan

"Set up the tabernacle according to the plan shown you on the mountain" - Exodus 26:30.

Moses was not given creative license to set up the tabernacle as he saw fit, for God had a plan for what this was to teach the Israelites and foreshadow Christ. Not only did the Lord direct Moses as to how he was to build the tabernacle, He also gave him directions how to set it up. If you need help with organizing your life and work, then the place to go is to God and trust His Spirit to lead you in the way you should go. **Are you drawing on all that God has for you as you organize your day, your work, and your life? Where is your organizational plan the weakest? Why do you think that is so? Is**

it out of fear? Is there someone God has placed in your life who can help you with this deficiency? *Lord, I don't want to over-spiritualize my work, expecting You to do what You have directed me to do. Yet I need Your help and input on how to organize my life! I trust You to send the right people and information into my world and I will carry out Your plan to the smallest detail.*

December 14
Holiness and Fruit

"For if you possess these qualities in increasing measure, they will keep you from being ineffective and unproductive in your knowledge of our Lord Jesus Christ" - 2 Peter 1:8.

The Greek words for ineffective and unproductive relate to being lazy and shunning the work that one has to do, not yielding the fruit that one ought to produce. Your knowledge of and relationship with Jesus should lead you to be productive. Goal-setting is one means by which that productivity can come to pass. **Are your holiness qualities leading you to good fruit? Are your goals helping you express this fruit? What new goals will stretch your faith and increase productivity as you grow in your knowledge of God?** *Lord, I don't just want to be holy, but holy **and** productive in Your will for my life. I have things in my heart that I have been hesitant to express. Help me overcome my hesitancy so I can commit to a course of action with goals and to persevere to see them accomplished.*

December 15
Family

"So Gideon took ten of his servants and did as the

Lord told him. But because he was afraid of his family and the townspeople, he did it at night rather than in the daytime" - Judges 6:27.

Gideon had faith to obey the Lord, but there was one major stumbling block for faith in his life, and that was his family. He did what God wanted in this instance, but he did so under the cover of darkness. The opposite of faith is not un-faith or unbelief, but rather fear. Gideon was afraid of what his family would think and say so he carried out a clandestine faith operation. **Of what are you afraid that is hindering your faith? Is your relationship with your family one that sustains and promotes your faith or hinders it? What are you prepared to do about that if the latter is the case?** *Lord, I love my family, but I am sometimes too concerned about what they will say and think. At times I also need them to need me, so I do things that perpetuate an unhealthy relationship that hinders my faith. Forgive me for putting my family before You and Your purposes for my life.*

December 16
Your Verse

"Open my eyes that I may see wonderful things in your law" - Psalm 119:18.

You probably have a verse or passage from Scripture that helps define your purpose, something that closely describes who you are and what you do best. The psalmist knew that God would have to open his eyes to see anything in the Word and you would do well to pray for the same thing. **How is your study of the Word going these days? Do you have a life-defining passage from the Bible? Do you have faith to**

discover one? Lord, I have lived my life as a person of your Word and now I need new insight from it as to who I am and what it is that You called me to do. Open my eyes to see the wonderful things the psalmist mentioned and then to use Your word to lead and guide me to purpose through the power of Your Spirit.

December 17
Next Year

"A discerning person keeps wisdom in view, but a fool's eyes wander to the ends of the earth"
- Proverbs 17:24.

Goals help you stay focused. In fact, they help you focus on something in the first place. Without them you tend to either daydream - which in this verse is described as your eyes wandering to the ends of the earth - or replicate what you already have and do every day. **Can you name goals that you achieved this year? Can you identify some on which you made significant progress? What about next year - what are your goals for the coming year and beyond?** Lord, I want to be realistic, but also set faith goals that are beyond my reach but within my capability of achieving with Your help. Help me to strike that proper balance. I thank You for what I was able to accomplish this year, but next year, I want more and will start to plan for that 'more' right now.

December 18
No Shortcuts

"A faithful person will be richly blessed, but one eager to get rich will not go unpunished"
- Proverbs 28:20.

When you discuss one who is faithful, it in part pertains to how they use their time. In this case, if you use your time to find shortcuts to success or productivity, you will certainly fail. If you identify your life values and devote your time to those day in and day out, year in and year out, you will find the kind of fulfillment and success you are seeking. **Have you spelled out the values that govern your life? Are you being faithful or true to your values through good use of your time? Are you looking for shortcuts of how to get where you want to go when there are none?** *Lord, I want to be known as a faithful person. I know that involves how I use my money, how well I follow through on commitments and how I use my time. I know what's important to me, now I must invest my time on those things to see them come to pass. Deliver me from seeking shortcuts to this lifelong process.*

December 19
Lifestyle

"And without faith it is impossible to please God, because anyone who comes to him must believe that he exists and that he rewards those who earnestly seek him" - Hebrews 11:6.

Faith is not an event; it is a lifestyle. Faith is not a parachute that you pull out in emergencies, it is to be your day-to-day walk with the Lord as you find and fulfill purpose, set and achieve goals, manage your time and organize your life and world around you. Without faith it is impossible to please God. That means with faith you can please Him. **Are you pleasing Him? Is faith a lifestyle for you or just something you use when you are backed into a corner and have no other options? What are you trusting the Lord for right now that, if**

He does not come through, you will look foolish?
Lord, I want to please You and there is no way to do that without trusting You and without faith. I confess that I often have faith when I have run out of options, but I see today that You desire a lifestyle of faith and not just an occasional excursion into faith. Forgive me for my unbelief as I venture forth in faith.

December 20
Details

"With this in mind, since I myself have carefully investigated everything from the beginning, I too decided to write an orderly account for you, most excellent Theophilus, so that you may know the certainty of the things you have been taught"
- Luke 1:3-4.

Luke was a scientist, of sorts, so he was accustomed to being meticulous in his work. When he went to write a gospel he organized his work carefully. First, he investigated thoroughly; then he decided to write his findings in an orderly, chronological format. Finally, he had so much material that he ended up writing his gospel and what we know to be the book of Acts. All throughout his work Luke evidenced a profound ability to organize his work and thoughts. **What about you? Do you invest the same attention to organizational detail in your work? What can you do to improve in the coming year?** *Lord, I see that when You use someone like me, there is no substitute for clear thought and organization. Success is never haphazard or accidental, but rather You work with and promote those who can keep Your call and work from being buried and lost in confusion and disorder. Help me to be able to handle the details well.*

December 21
Clarity

"(Yes, I also baptized the household of Stephanas; beyond that, I don't remember if I baptized anyone else.) For Christ did not send me to baptize, but to preach the gospel—not with wisdom and eloquence, lest the cross of Christ be emptied of its power"
- 1 Corinthians 1:16-17.

You have to admire and respect what Paul accomplished and the impact he had. All that did not happen by accident. Paul had exceptional clarity as to who he was, what he was to do and what he was *not* to do, as evidenced by these verses. He also had wisdom as to how to preach the gospel to the Gentiles and he walked in that purpose until his death. God wants you to have what Paul had - awareness - and do what he did - purpose. **Do you have the kind of awareness that Paul had? Are you acting on it? Do you have wisdom for how you are to carry out the purpose for your life?** *Lord, I want what Paul had! I want and need clarity into who I am and what You want me to do. Then I need wisdom so I can fulfill my purpose with the kind of efficiency and effectiveness Paul had. You promised if I asked for wisdom, You would give it, so I'm asking and thanking You in advance.*

December 22
Tree of Life

"Hope deferred makes the heart sick, but a longing fulfilled is a tree of life"
- Proverbs 13:12.

There are undoubtedly many things in your heart, many

things you have said you would like to do one day. In the words of the wisdom writer, you have a longing. When you set a goal and achieve it, you find life and that life is similar in terminology to the tree of life that was mentioned in the Garden of Eden. So when you set and reach goals you are cooperating with God's original plan for mankind to exercise dominion over the things of earth. If you don't set goals then you are deferring your hope. You will be heartsick and that can lead to physical illness as well. **As you approach the New Year why not take some time today and set some goals?** *Lord, I want to function as You created me to do, and part of that is to achieve the things that are in my heart to do and be. I understand that goal setting is not optional in that process, so I commit to put down in writing the hopes I have in my heart and work diligently to make them happen.*

December 23
Spending Time

"You yourselves know that these hands of mine have supplied my own needs and the needs of my companions" - Acts 20:34.

Paul had a value not to be a financial burden on his converts so that the gospel would not be criticized or connected to traveling teachers common in his day. He did not just talk or think about that value. That value impacted his time and determined how he was going to spend the hours in his day. Paul did not work first and foremost to make money; he worked both to express his values and also to support and further his apostolic mission. **How are you spending your time? Is your time management values-driven or do you sell yourself to the loudest, most urgent bidder? Why do** you work and do what you do? Is it simply to make money?** If so, then money is your highest value! **Is that how you want it to be remembered?** *Lord, I often say 'it's not about the money,' but then proceed to invest my precious time like it's all about the money. I know I need money, but I need purpose more and therefore I must learn to spend my time to support my purpose, not my eating habits. I need to change my thinking where my time is concerned.*

December 24
A Man Named Nehemiah

"The men of Jericho built the adjoining section, and Zakkur son of Imri built next to them. The Fish Gate was rebuilt by the sons of Hassenaah. They laid its beams and put its doors and bolts and bars in place" - Nehemiah 3:2-3.

Nehemiah's purpose was to rebuild Jerusalem. That was a big task involving many people; some friendly to his cause, some not. He had to give significant thought to how he was going to organize his effort and the efforts in these verses provide just a glimpse from God's inspired Word of who did what to rebuild the wall, the first step in Nehemiah's purpose plan. **What thought have you given to how you will achieve your purpose work? How are you organizing your world to make it happen? What changes do you need to make to be more effective and fruitful?** *Lord, I have had big dreams and plans, but often they break down in the implementation phase. In other words, I have not known how, and sometimes not wanted, to make the changes necessary to rearrange my world to fulfill my purpose. Help me to do so and help me to help others as well so that our purpose quests will come to fruition.*

December 25
Faith Scroll

"Then those who feared the Lord talked with each other, and the Lord listened and heard. A scroll of remembrance was written in his presence concerning those who feared the Lord and honored his name" - Malachi 3:16.

The Lord is listening to your conversations with yourself and with others. We see from Hebrews 11 that you must talk faith to please God, and Hebrews 11 contains a scroll of remembrance for those who distinguished themselves in faith. The Lord is obviously still adding to that scroll and your name can be on it! **Is God enjoying listening in on your conversations these days? Are you having faith discussions with others of what you can do in faith, or what you can't do in unbelief? Are you eager to have your name enrolled in the faith hall of fame?** *Lord, I want to be registered on your faith scroll, but I see that I have to earn my way onto that list by honoring You. The best way I know to honor You is to put my trust in You, so I want to talk and live faith, so that You will take notice. I commit to talk faith in the coming year both to myself and to others.*

December 26
Purpose Food

"Whoever has ears, let them hear what the Spirit says to the churches. To the one who is victorious, I will give some of the hidden manna. I will also give that person a white stone with a new name written on it, known only to the one who receives it" - Revelation 2:17.

Purpose is hidden manna - something that energizes and sustains you and nobody else. (This resembles Jesus' remark that He had food to eat about which His disciples knew nothing.) Your purpose is also like the white stone mentioned in this verse that has a title or description on it that is only meaningful (and sometimes only visible) to you alone. **What activity 'feeds' you, giving you meaning and energy? What statement describes your purpose and is a message from heaven about your new purpose identity? What have you discovered about your purpose this past year that only became 'visible' to you as you sought and prayed?** *Lord, I thank You for the power of purpose in my life. It is truly a gift from heaven that is obvious to me while meaningless and invisible to most others. It is also 'bread from heaven' that strengthens me with supernatural power on a daily basis. Thank You for the purpose progress I made this past year!*

December 27
Thorns and Thistles

"Land that drinks in the rain often falling on it and that produces a crop useful to those for whom it is farmed receives the blessing of God. But land that produces thorns and thistles is worthless and is in danger of being cursed. In the end it will be burned" - Hebrews 6:7-8.

Productivity and fruitfulness are a constant theme and expectation in the Bible for those who know the Lord. You have rain falling on your life in the form of God's grace, mercy, creative inspiration and insight. What's more, you are exposed to the insight and encouragement of God's word. You therefore have a mandate to produce a crop useful to the Lord and others.

There is no better way to insure this crop of fruit than to set and persevere in your goals that are specific and marinated in faith. **What are your goals for next year? For the next five years? For the next ten? Is your fruit what you are not doing or what God has put in your heart to do?** *Lord, I don't want You to mark me 'useless ground' because I produce thorns and thistles. My objective is to produce a crop that will impress even You (if that's possible). And I don't only want to achieve easy within-my-reach goals, but ones that require my absolute faith and trust in Your provision and help.*

December 28
Priorities-Driven

"As was his custom, Paul went into the synagogue, and on three Sabbath days he reasoned with them from the Scriptures" - Acts 17:2.

Paul worked full-time to meet the needs of his team, but spent his off day fulfilling his purpose of taking the gospel to the Gentiles. He started that purpose process in each city by visiting synagogues where he would find interested Jews and Gentiles. Paul followed his priorities carefully and did not use free time to do nothing, but used it to fulfill his purpose. **Have you identified your priorities? Are you following them by devoting your time to them in order of importance? Do you have faith that if you follow your priorities and do what you feel led to do God will multiply your efforts?** *Lord, it seems that every day time slips away before I can get to the most important things. Some of those things have languished for years in my heart, but no more. Today I will identify my priorities and then, with Your help, discover how I can faithfully follow those priorities in my daily use of time.*

December 29
Big

"All the men assigned to the camp of Judah, according to their divisions, number 186,400. They will set out first" - Numbers 2:9.

God is not intimidated by size. It is as easy for Him to lead, administer and provide for a million as it is a hundred. If God is not overwhelmed then you should not be either. Yet at times it is possible to resist 'big' or even consider it unspiritual. You don't want to be working toward 'small' when God has 'big' in mind. Then you are resisting His plan for your family, ministry or business. **Are you intimidated by the thoughts of overseeing something large? Are you actively working to keep your world small and manageable by your current skill? Can you understand why God may want 'big'?**
Lord, I admit that I am biased against big at times because it will stretch my comfort zone beyond what I think is appropriate. Forgive me where I have limited Your work and my involvement in it. My vision and faith are too small and that is why I work to shrink my world instead of expanding my capacity.

December 30
Totally His

"For the eyes of the Lord range throughout the earth to strengthen those whose hearts are fully committed to him" - 2 Chronicles 16:9.

When you are fully committed to the Lord, you can count on Him finding you and strengthening you in the work you are doing. To be fully committed, you must embark on the walk of faith in your family, work and ministry.

That doesn't mean you are perfect, but that your first thoughts and plans are of the Lord and what He would want you to do on purpose. **Do you believe that God is searching for those who are completely His? Do you think you can be one of those people? What heart changes should you make in the coming year for God to search and find you?** *Lord, I read this verse and it stirs my heart, for I want to be someone whom You can consider totally committed to You. I surrender my life's agenda to You and I submit to Your purpose and will for my life. I will not allow family or circumstances to deter me in the coming year, with Your help, of course.*

December 31
Jesus' Help

"It is too small a thing for you to be my servant to restore the tribes of Jacob and bring back those of Israel I have kept. I will also make you a light for the Gentiles, that my salvation may reach to the ends of the earth" - Isaiah 49:6

Of course, this prophecy refers to Jesus and His mission. Because Jesus had purpose, You also have purpose. You can rely on Him to help fulfill yours because He fulfilled His. What's more, God can use you mightily to do more and be more than you thought possible, all by His grace. **Are you thinking big for the coming year? Are you thinking big in regards to your purpose? Have you set lofty goals that require God's power to achieve?** *Lord, I thank You for this String of Pearls this past year. I have been challenged to be and do more and today's verse is in keeping with that theme. I submit myself to do whatever You want, without false humility or second thoughts. I want to be a person of purpose and I submit myself to Your plan for my life.*

CONCLUSION

When I started writing my Purpose Pearls at the beginning of the year, I was skeptical that I would be able to maintain the daily regimen. It's not that I doubted my commitment to write every day, but I was not sure I would able to find 366 verses or passages that related to the five Gold Mine Principles of purpose, goals, time management, organization and faith. As I finished, I had material left over that I didn't use.

My relationship with these five Principles began in 1985 and continues to grow stronger and more meaningful. These Principles are the foundation in my own personal productivity, and I have applied them again and again in meetings with people all over the globe. Purpose continues to grow in significance as evidenced by the steady stream of books and other resources trumpeting its importance and, as I get older, the issue of time management becomes more and more important. I spend a lot of time organizing my world – computer documents, papers, books, travel – and goals are more important to my leadership role than ever. And of course, all of those Principles are marinated in the fifth Principle, which is faith, for without faith, it's impossible to please God.

Yet my hope is not that you continue to study these five Principles but rather find ways to apply them in your daily life and walk with the Lord. Believers are people of the Word and words are important to us. Thus when we have said something sincerely, we have a sense of finality, like we have done something, when in fact we have not. We must move beyond being good talkers to effective doers as Jesus Himself stated in John 13:17: "Now that you know these things, you will be blessed if you do them."

My hope is that you will take these individual Pearls presented in this book and string them together, combining them into attractive 'jewelry' that you can wear and display. Put some goal Pearls with some time management Pearls, and then finish off your work with some faith Pearls and, voila, you will have something attractive that looks good on you. Then wear it well, but keep working on putting together new combinations in creative expressions of your God-given purpose.

I don't know how many days I have remaining on earth, but I am committed to continue doing what I have urged you to do – design strings of Pearls that will bring glory to God and satisfaction to my soul. If I can help you string your Pearls, don't hesitate to contact me or check out my ongoing body of purpose work at www.purposequest.com. Thank you for faithfully reading these Pearls and may they continue to provide you with motivation and practical tips on how to be a more purposeful and productive person.

A String Of Pearls

Scripture References

A String of Pearls

Genesis
1:2 April 9
1:5 September 9
1:10 September 10
1:12 September 11
1:28 June 20
2:18 June 21
13:17 November 29
17:49 September 6
24:3-4 August 16
24:12-14 August 17
37:5 November 1
37:8 November 2
37:10-11 November 3
37:14b-17 July 19
41:48 September 5
42:8-9 July 18
50:26 July 17

Exodus
3:3 January 18
18:14 March 24
18:14 September 14
18:17-18 March 25
18:18 September 15
18:19 March 26
18:20 March 27
18:21 March 28
18:23 March 29
18:24 September 16
23:14 September 29
25:9 December 11
26:30 December 13
31:1-2 January 17
31:4-5 January 19
31:6 January 20
31:11 January 21

Numbers
2:9 December 29
8:13 August 20
10:5 September 13
11:28 November 24
14:34 August 19
27:18 November 25

Judges
6:12 November 12
6:27 December 15
13:5 November 26

Joshua
10:6-7 March 12
10:8-9 March 13
10:10-11 March 14
10:12-13 March 15

Joshua (cont.)
10:13b-14 March 16
10:17 March 17
10:20 March 18

Ruth
1:16 December 8

1 Samuel
1:11 November 28
14:1 February 20
14:3 February 21
14:4 February 22
14:6 February 23
14:7 February 24
14:8-10 February 25
14:13-14 February 26
14:18-19 February 27
14:22 February 28
14:23 February 1
16:13 November 17
17:20 July 4
17:24 July 5
17:25 July 6
17:28 July 7
17:32 July 8
17:33 July 9
17:37-40 July 10
17:40 July 11
17:46 December 6
17:49 December 7
23:17 November 30

2 Samuel
5:8 May 23

1 Kings
3:9 November 22
4:1-3 September 19
4:7 September 20
4:32-34 July 24
6:38 July 22
7:1 July 23
10:1 April 11
10:2 April 12
10:3 April 13
10:4 July 25
10:4-5 April 14
10:6-7 April 15
10:9 April 16
10:11-12 April 17
12:10 September 17
19:15-16 March 21
19:20 December 4
19;21 March 22

2 Kings
2:13 November 21
3:11 November 20
7:7 April 25
18:37 September 18

1 Chronicles
11:6 February 14
11:20 September 4
12:32 March 4
28:11 September 21

2 Chronicles
16:9 December 30

Esther
2:7 November 7
3:9 November 8
4:14 November 9

Nehemiah
1:4 November 13
2:6 August 30
3:2-3 December 24
3:38 September 1
4:21 September 2
5:18 November 15
6:15 August 31
8:10 November 14
13:14, 22 November 16

Job
25:2 September 28

Psalms
1:1-2 September 26
50:17 August 11
50:17 September 25
119:18 December 16

Proverbs
1:1-2 July 20
1:5 August 14
2:2 June 5
2:3-4 June 6
2:4 August 12
2:5 June 7
3:19 August 5
3:26 July 14
4:25 June 1
4:21 June 2
5:10 August 18
6:6-8 April 2
6:9 August 7
6:9-11 March 31
6:10 August 8

294

Scripture References

Proverbs (cont.)
6:11	August 9
8:1	August 13
8:29-31	April 22
9:1-2	September 27
9:11	August 4
10:4	February 15
10:5	March 30
12:11	February 19
13:4	February 17
13:12	December 22
13:20	August 15
14:4	April 18
14:4	April 24
14:23	February 13
14:23	July 13
14:28	April 7
16:3	July 15
16:3	July 16
16:4	June 4
17:24	December 17
18:1	June 9
18:9	July 26
19:8	June 11
20:11	July 12
21:5	February 12
22:19	May 10
24:7	June 3
24:27	March 7
25:1	July 21
25:2	June 8
25:19	August 6
28:19	June 10
28:20	December 18
29:18	April 19
30:27	April 1

Ecclesiastes
3:1-3	March 3
10:10	March 2
12:9	September 3

Isaiah
6:5	November 18
6:8	November 19
49:6	December 31

Jeremiah
1:5	June 16

Daniel
2:20b-22	November 11
2:49	September 7
6:4	September 8

Amos
1:1	December 9

Habakkuk
2:1-3	February 11
2:2-3	April 27
2:4	May 24

Malachi
3:16	December 25

Matthew
3:3	June 14
3:3	June 15
4:19	November 27
6:30	October 1
6:33	March 8
8:10	October 2
8:26	October 3
9:2	October 4
13:58	October 5
14:31	October 6
15:28	October 7
16:8-9	October 9
17:19-20	October 10
20:28	November 6
21:21	October 11

Mark
3:20	August 22
4:40	October 11
5:36	October 17
6:6	October 12
6:31-34	August 25
8:27	December 10
9:24	October 18
11:22	October 13
11:24	May 26
11:24	October 19

Luke
1:3-4	December 20
1:45	October 20
1:45	November 10
3:11	April 10
4:16-21	June 27
5:5	August 23
6:12-13	August 24
7:30	December 1
8:13	October 21
8:25	October 14
8:50	October 22
12:28	October 16
16:10	April 28
16:11	April 29
16:12	April 30

Luke (cont.)
17:5	October 15
19:10	November 4
22:67	October 29
23:42-43	August 26
24:11	October 30
24:25-26	October 31

John
4:6-7	January 31
4:7	June 18
7:7-8	December 3
7:17	March 5
7:38	October 23
9:38	October 24
12:37	October 25
13:17	March 6
14:1	October 26
14:11	October 27
17:4	June 30
19:27	October 28
20:6-7	December 2

Acts
3:18	April 6
4:36	June 28
4:37	June 29
6:1	January 1
6:2	January 2
6:3-4	January 3
6:4	January 4
6:5	January 5
6:6	January 6
6:7	January 7
7:20	January 23
7:25	January 22
9:36	January 8
9:39	January 8
9:40	January 10
9:42	January 11
10:38	June 17
13:46	August 3
17:2	December 28
18:2-3	January 28
18:4	March 9
18:9	January 25
20:7	September 24
20:11	April 23
20:34	December 23
20:34-35	August 1
22:3	December 5
22:10	January 13
22:17-18	January 14
22:19	January 15
22:21	January 16
27:23-24	January 26

Acts (cont.)
28:30-31 January 27

Romans
4:19 May 16
4:20-21 May 17
10:17 May 22
14:23 May 1
15:20 August 2
15:20-21 February 9
15:23-24 February 10

1 Corinthians
1:16-17 December 21
9:12 March 10
12:28 September 12
14:7-8 June 19
14:33 April 3
14:33 April 8
15:10 March 19
15:10 July 1
15:10 July 2
15:10 July 3
15:46 April 21
16:9 June 22
16:9 June 23

2 Corinthians
4:13 May 18
5:7 May 19
5:9 February 6
6:1 July 27
6:4-5 August 29
8:14-15 February 7
8:19 September 22
8:20 September 23
11:27-28 March 20

Galatians
2:7 January 24
2:7-9 June 12
2:7-9 June 12

Ephesians
1:19-20 July 28
3:7 January 30
3:7 July 29
3:16 July 30
3:20 July 31
5:15-16 March 1

Philippians
2:13 April 20
3:14 February 1
3:14 February 2
3:14 February 3

Philippians (cont.)
3:14 February 4
4:13 June 25
4:13 June 26

Colossians
1:28-29 February 18
2:2 February 5
4:13 August 21
4:14 January 29

2 Timothy
1:7 April 4
4:13 April 5

Titus
1:5 April 26

Hebrews
1:9 June 24
3:12 December 12
6:7-8 December 27
10:22 May 29
10:24 May 30
10:24 May 31
10:38 May 27
10:39 May 28
11:1 May 5
11:3 May 6
11:4 May 7
11:6 May 2
11:6 May 3
11:6 December 19
11:8 May 9
11:9b May 11
11:10 May 12
11:11 May 13
11:13 May 14
11:14 May 20
11:23 May 25
12:1-2 May 4
12:2 February 8

James
2:17 May 15
2:18 May 21

2 Peter
1:8 December 14
3:8 August 10

1 John
3:8 November 5

Revelation
1:9-10a August 27
1:19 August 28
2:17 December 26
5:10 March 24

ABOUT THE AUTHOR

John Stanko is the founder and president of PurposeQuest International, which creates resources and tools to help people around the world clarify their purpose and order their lives. He is a sought-after conference speaker and consultant, and his website and blog are popular sites where people go to better understand who they are and how to be more productive.

John resides in Pittsburgh, PA and earned his Doctor of Ministry from Reformed Presbyterian Theological Seminary. You can stay in touch with John's world through the following sites and radio shows:

www.purposequest.com

www.johnstanko.us

www.stankobiblestudy.com

www.stankomondaymemo.com

www.blogtalkradio.com/acacthreads

www.blogtalkradio.com/genevacollegemsol

or via email at johnstanko@gmail.com

John also does extensive relief and community development work in Kenya. You can see some of his projects at www.purposequest.com/contributions.

PurposeQuest International
PO Box 8882
Pittsburgh, PA 15221-0882

OTHER BOOKS BY JOHN STANKO

Life is a Gold Mine

I Wrote This Book on PurposeQuest

A Daily Dose of Proverbs

A Daily Taste of Proverbs

Strictly Business

Unlocking the Power of Your PurposeQuest

Beyond Purpose

The Faith Files: Volume One

The Faith Files: Volume Two

The Faith Files: Volume Three

Changing the Way We Do Church

The Revelation Project

The Price of Leadership

What Would Jesus Ask You Today?

Urban Heroes: Volume One

Urban Heroes: Volume Two

www.ingramcontent.com/pod-product-compliance
Lightning Source LLC
LaVergne TN
LVHW051543070426
835507LV00021B/2384